300 Monologues

By
Vin Morreale, Jr.

Cover Design by
Amanda Michelle Morreale

ISBN 978-0-9991473-3-7

PRESS

academyartspress.com

TABLE OF CONTENTS

The Purpose Of This Book   iii

A Unique Artform   v

Dramatic Monologues   1- 100

Comedic Monologues   101 – 173

For permission to use any of these monologues in a performance, and for school or multi-book discounts, please email vin@academyarts.com

Want to sharpen your acting skills, plus have a chance to showcase your talent to a national audience?

Visit 300monologues.com

The Purpose of This Book

As both a working director and casting director for stage, screen and commercials, I have seen far too many strong actors crash and burn during the audition process, often due to their choice of audition pieces. Either they were unprepared with a monologue when requested, or the one they chose to perform gave no indication they could match the role being cast.

The night before an audition is never the time to start learning a monologue. Every actor should have two or more that they have memorized and rehearsed extensively; at least one dramatic and one comedic to prove they can fit comfortably in these worlds. The monologues you choose to make your own can also enhance or detract from your ability to win a role. If the role is contemporary, a well-delivered Shakespeare soliloquy gives the casting director no indication you can handle the part. If we are casting for a comedy, your ability to cry on cue may be wasted.

There are a number of standard monologues that have been done to death. If I never see another actor performing the "You can't handle the truth!" monologue from A Few Good Men, I will be ecstatic. It is worth studying this exceptional piece of writing, but I suggest you do not carry it into the audition room. Bringing a classic monologue to an audition means you are actually competing with the actor who made that specific piece of theater so iconic. Unless you are vastly superior to Jack Nicholson in your delivery, which is unlikely, your performance will suffer in comparison.

When casting, I always prefer a fresh piece of writing that I have never heard before. It will hold my attention and help you stand out from the crowd.

Think of it this way... if you heard the same joke thirty times, it doesn't matter how funny it is, or how well it was told. Part of your brain goes to sleep each additional time you hear it.

I remember one long casting day, where five different actors used the same monologue for their audition. As you can imagine, none of them got the part.

Years ago, I chose to differentiate my Burning Up The Stage Acting Workshops by always creating new monologues and scenes for every class. Participants always had something fresh and original to play with, which gave me a greater sense of their ability to develop a character, instead of copying a classic performance by a movie star. This always added an exciting dimension to the workshops, and gave each actor more confidence in making choices, instead of simple mimicry.

Some of the enclosed monologues I wrote for specific students, who needed to reach beyond their comfort zone, or risk being forever typecast. A shy actor may have had difficulty expressing anger or flirtatiousness, so I would create pieces that would challenge him or her to expand their skills beyond their fears, and give them confidence in playing an unaccustomed role. And once you push past your fears and self-criticism to tackle a character so unlike your natural personality, you begin to realize how versatile a performer you can truly be.

So whether you are an actor seeking to book more jobs and reach beyond your self-imposed limitations, a teacher looking to challenge your students with more diverse material, or simply someone who enjoys reading scripts, I hope you enjoy these 300 Monologues as much as I enjoyed writing them.

Vin Morreale, Jr.

A Unique Artform

There are few artforms as versatile and effective as the monologue. It is equally powerful in stage, screen and radio, often comprising the most memorable moments of a movie or stage play. More people recognize the classic line, "To be or not to be" than can describe the basic plot of Hamlet or name another character besides the Danish prince.

Monologues are also able to insert themselves into virtually any situation. They can add a moment of argument or internal disclosure within a rapid-fire dialogue scene. They can serve as conscious narration for a larger work, as in a one-person play, or stand alone as the briefest of glimpses into a character's thoughts or feelings. They can be used to communicate with others, talk to ourselves, or in some cases, break the fourth wall as an aside and speak directly to the audience. One might even say the vast majority of popular songs are simply monologues set to music.

In terms of content, monologues can be either inadvertently revealing or self-deceiving, depending on how aware your character may be of his or her own thoughts. That is why this unique artform can be so riveting, because even the words we choose to speak can subtly disclose the vast spiderweb of lies or truths we tell ourselves, in order to remain sane in a world of near continuous interactions. As such, they may let the very foundations of our personality slip out, whether we want them to or not.

We tend to think of ourselves as having a fairly clear picture of who we are, as if it is some image as stable as our physical appearance. Every event, every relationship, every memory helps us build or fortify this image. Yet, our fears, defenses, hopes and dreams constantly churn beneath the surface, making us little more than messy sacks of jumbled emotions and ideas, that can change shape with even the slightest prodding from external forces. A smile from a stranger can lift our spirits as easily as a single unkind word from someone we love can initiate a dark spiral of despair.

So, what makes a good monologue? For me, it is the ability to quickly reveal more than the character intends, or even understands about his or her own beliefs. The unveiling or the mask. Or occasionally both.

The best monologues let us peek behind the curtain to see what clunky mechanisms drive our character forward. An outwardly expressed inner whisper we hope no one else hears. An inadvertent confession. An involuntary divulging. A solitary conversation. Or a personality condensed. As if the character speaking has ripped open his chest to reveal something he hoped would remain forever hidden.

But most of all, they should be interesting, and fun to watch.

The 300 monologues contained in this book show a wide range of emotions and self-delusions. For perfect people are, well…boring. It is all our flaws and foolishness that make us both human and relatable.

With the exception of a few of the simpler comedic pieces, I have tried to build at least two or three different emotions into every monologue. Your job as an actor is to identify each emotion, and subtly navigate the transitions between them in a way that is most honest to the character you are portraying. And that is the most important aspect of a monologue. You are not simply reciting lines; you are creating a character. Hopefully, one that touches the heart or imagination of your audience. To do this, you must find something to like about that character, even the most evil or inept ones. And make their words uniquely personal in your performance.

If all the above seems too analytical, throw it away. Enjoy the process. Celebrate the words, even when they are silly or awkwardly constructed. For you must see your characters as real, in order to bring them to life for your audience. Actors who take themselves too seriously often squeeze the joy out of the theater experience. Challenge yourself with characters that are nothing like you perceive yourself to be, and you just may find more things in common with them than you can imagine.

Dramatic Monologues

1.

So that's it?

Thirty years with the same company. Only took three sick days in all that time. Staying late, doing everything they asked of me, only to get kicked to the curb because the bottom line took a hit this quarter? Why don't you sell off one of those private jets nobody uses? Or cut back on the annual bonus for all the upper management? Each of those guys makes more in a week than I get paid for an entire year! But that ain't gonna happen, is it?

You know, when I started here thirty years ago, this company cared more about people than profits. I'm not talking any socialist crap here. I know how business works. But there has to be a balance. Because you and me and Reggie there, Paul and Eduardo in Shipping, Audrey and Laticia in Marketing, Tim in Sales, and Ginger in Accounting... we *are* this company. We *are* your bottom line. When you lose sight of that, then everything we worked for, everything your grandfather tried so hard to build when he started this company, it's all just numbers on a page. Nothing more than that.

Okay, I've said my piece.

I'll go clean out my desk now.

2.

You want the truth? All right. I'm scared. I admit it. It may seem like a little surgery to you, but it's a knife. They are planning to cut me open to look and see if there's anything in there they don't want to see. And all that scares the hell out of me. Y'know, back when I was a kid, I thought my dad was the strongest man in the world. He was big and loud, and as tough as an alligator on steroids. He had arms bigger than most people's legs. He'd walk into a room and just own the place. Everybody gave him respect, or they were smart enough to stay out of his way. Even I was afraid of him, though I knew he'd never hurt me. Unless maybe, a whipping now and then, which I deserved. Then when I was ten, he went into the hospital for a minor operation. 'Nothing serious,' he laughed. 'Don't worry,' he told my mom. 'Nothing to it at all.' So, they put him under and opened him up. But what they found was way more than they expected, so the doctors poked around and just closed him back up again. There was nothing they could do. They came out to tell my mom, so she could break the news to my dad when he woke up. But he never did. Something about the anesthesia, or the shock to the body. Or maybe, even though he was asleep, he knew what was ahead of him, and didn't want to put my mom and me through all that. So, the biggest, toughest man I ever knew was taken down by a little operation. Now tell me…
What chance do I have?

3.

Kristen asked me if we could go over to Grandma's
house for supper tonight. She always loved the way
Grandma made her special soup and home-made bread.
The way her house filled up with those warm, delicious
scents that always made you feel like you were home.
Kristen wanted to show Grandma a picture she drew in
Kindergarten. It was a picture of Grandma cooking.
I knelt down beside Kristen and kissed her little hands. I
told her we can't go over Grandma's house for supper
anymore. I reminded her that Grandma is an angel now.
That God needed her to up in heaven. He needed her to
bake bread for Jesus and the other angels. Kristen was
silent for a moment. "I forgot," she said, and shrugged
her little shoulders. She looked down at her little
drawing. Then she asked me a question that tore my
heart in two. "Mommy... does all heaven smell as good as
Grandma's kitchen?" All I could do was hug her until I
stopped crying.

4.

You ask me what I want? It's simple. All I want is fifteen
minutes of forever. Even if it's a lie. Even if we both
know we have no future together. Even if it's all just one
sadly beautiful illusion we both buy into. Just fifteen
minutes with no pain. No fear. No loneliness. Fifteen
minutes of forever. Is that so much to ask?

5.

I'm going up to bed now. You can sleep on the sofa or grab the sleeping bag and lay down on the floor in the porch. In fact, you can sleep in the garbage disposal for all I care. Just know this…that was the very last time you will EVER lay your hands on me again. I don't care if it is all the pressure at work, or your stupid temper, or that quart of Wild Turkey you cling to like it's your last friend on Earth… If you ever dare lay hands on me again, I swear to God, I will shred you in your sleep. And believe me, no amount of Wild Turkey will help ease that pain. So, I'm going to bed now. And you…you can go somewhere and curl up and die for all I care. Just turn out the lights before you do.

6.

I don't belong here. I don't know why, but I don't. I'm like that one extra piece that gets mixed in from another puzzle. It just won't fit right, no matter what you do. I'm always the odd one out. The one who says all the wrong things. Whose feelings don't match. Who makes everyone else uncomfortable…nobody more than himself. People pretend not to notice, but they do. I don't belong here. I never did. I just pray that there is somehow, somewhere I fit in. Somewhere I belong. Somewhere else...

7.

You are a great entertainer. Really. The stories you tell. The maximum amount of sympathy you squeeze out of every sentence. Your well-placed sighs of exhaustion. Listening to you, I almost could believe how hard it was for you. How difficult your life must have been all those years. Unfortunately for you, I was there. I know what really happened. And it's all I can do to keep from laughing every time you rewrite history to make yourself the martyr of the moment. The star of every event. Most people live on air, food and water. You thrive on pity. So, if it makes you happy to convince people who have gone through so much more than you. People who have experienced real tragedy in their lives. If you need so desperately to make all of them feel sorry for you…that's fine. But I know better.

8.

You cried in your sleep last night. The way you do every night around 3:30 in the morning. You don't even know you do it. Don't know you've done it every night since Robbie…Since he… It's never enough to wake you. One soft, strangled moan in the darkness. Your shoulders shake and then go deathly still. Three silent tears fall from your cheek to the pillow. One…two…three… Then you're back to sleep again, dreaming of somewhere else. A place without pain. The kind of place that only exists in dreams.
And I envy you for it.

9.

What makes a relationship work? Perspective. Seeing the world through her eyes, instead of your own. You know, we all tend to think we are such a great catch. If only we could get free of this person, there would be a hundred eager lovers knocking at our door. Smarter and richer and prettier people would suddenly notice us and give up everything they have to be with us instead. That's the way we imagine it. That's what we'd like to think. Now look at it through her eyes… She sees a rumpled, complaining lump drag his sorry butt out of bed every morning. Bad breath and ridiculous pillow hair, you stumble to the bathroom; yawning, scratching and farting all the way. You're older than you believe you look. Saggier than you care to admit. And nowhere near as cheerful or fun to be around as you imagine yourself to be. But you stare into that mirror and somehow see a superstar buried under all those wrinkles, pounds and complaints. And while you cloud your bleary eyes with self-delusion, the person who stuck by your side all those years is thinking…if only she could get free of you…If only you were gone, there would be a hundred eager lovers knocking at her door. Smarter, richer, prettier and younger, instead of an angry old slob spending too much time hunkered over that bathroom mirror.

Perspective… You should be thanking God that she doesn't act on it. Because you're not really all that great a catch. The truth is you're the first one they'd throw back.

10.

It's funny. That's the first question they always ask. "Why are you doing this?" Like knowing is somehow going to make it easier for them. Trust me. It won't. The other thing they always say is "Please, I have a family!" Every time. Just like clockwork. "Why are you doing this?" and "Please, I have a family!" As if that's going to make a difference. But let me tell you a little secret… Everybody has a family. Everybody is somebody's mother, father, son or daughter, brother, sister, or third cousin twice removed. Don't make one bit of difference. You're still gonna die. It doesn't even matter why. Maybe you just screwed up. Made the wrong people angry. I'm getting paid a lot of money...
But you wanna know the real reason I'm doing this? The real reason is…I enjoy it. I really do. Some people like to camp, watch football, or do crossword puzzles. Me? I like to squeeze the life out of another human being. Sucks for you, doesn't it?

11.

It was like nothing else I ever saw. There was so much courage. So much compassion. Just thinking about it now makes me want to cry. In the middle of all that hatred, all that violence, she stood up. Brushed her hair back. Looked him straight in the eye, and then she…forgave him. Just like that. After all he did, she forgave him.
And none of us have been the same since…

12.

I wish it was different. You. Me. All of this...

I wish we were free to find out if there was something really there. Or if we were just reaching out to each other out of disappointment and loneliness.

Maybe it's more than that. I just don't know anymore...

Most people have no idea how easy it is to sleepwalk through a seemingly perfect life...marriage, kids, and career. Nice house, decent car, summer vacations at the lake...and still feel completely hollow and meaningless.

To have everything you ever thought you wanted, yet still have to drag yourself out of bed each morning. Force yourself to smile. To pretend like the sheer dark emptiness of it all isn't crushing the life right out of you. But you knew. I could see it in your eyes. You understood.

So maybe this is nothing more than that. Two lost and drowning people grabbing for the same life raft, and suddenly realizing they are not completely alone in that big, empty ocean of disappointment. And there's nothing they can do about it. The life raft is an illusion. So is any hope of a way out. They're lives are perfect, and each is doomed to drown alone.

I wish it was different.

You. Me. All of this.

I just wish it was different...

13.

I don't accept this. No. This is completely unacceptable. You are not the one who decides when this relationship is over. You are not the one who leaves first. That's what I do. What I've always done. I am not the one who gets broken up with. I do not get dumped. Ever. It's not me who ends up crying all night, hugging my tear-stained pillow, praying you'll give me another chance. You'll never see me leaving all those pitiful, pleading messages on your phone, wondering what I did wrong, and saying I'll do anything to get you to take me back. I don't do depression. I don't do desperation. That's not who I am. So, no, you can't leave. You can't break my heart like this. Not now. Not ever. Understand?

14.

The night before my son left for college, I cooked dinner as usual. No surprises. I've had more than enough surprises these last few months. My baby. This eager young man I called my son...was staring his future full in the face...and leaving me behind. In my head, I knew he was just doing what he had to do to become a man...but in my heart, he was rejecting me and everything I stood for. I gave eighteen years of my life to make him safe, strong and secure...and now he was leaving me behind. Eighteen frustrating and wonderful years...
And all I would have left to hold onto was this one, last supper...

15.

Have you ever imagined what it'd be like to meet your parents when they were younger? When they weren't so bent and burdened by mortgages and bills and jobs and...well, us? How much fun they must have been without all those worries. How different they must have looked with the future free and clear ahead of them. I think about that sometimes, and it makes me smile. Then I think about thirty or forty years from now. When our kids aren't those crazy pinballs of energy careening over the house. When instead of their infectious giggles and silly stories, they're slow and serious and struggling with the same bills, debts, fears and worries we all face. The twinkles in their eyes turned gray, and their smiles only turned on by humorless comedies and weekends with friends they can't stand. I think about that sometimes. My kids all grown up. And it breaks my heart.

16.

I don't care what you believe, just believe in something. Believe in God, second chances, the power of love, or helping your fellow man. Just believe in something more than yourself. Otherwise you're just taking up real estate. Sucking in oxygen better spent on someone with a purpose. And your life becomes nothing more than a video game hero whose timer is running down. So, stop your whining and come up with a reason to live. And a reason to be happy. It just takes a little faith.

17.

I can't hate him. I wish I could, but I can't. It'd make everything so much easier if I could walk away, not even looking back. Let the last image he has of me be the love of his life walking out the door, not even caring enough to turn around…or say goodbye. But then I see how sad he is…how much pain he's holding inside him, and then I feel… I don't know…sorry for him, I guess. I mean, how can I tear him apart, when he does it to himself every minute of every hour of every day? They say you only hurt the ones you love, and maybe that's true. But once you love somebody, once you are totally committed to them with heart and soul and everything you have… then watching them suffer, watching them throw away their lives, is worse than any pain they could ever put you through… At least that's what I think…

18.

So that's your big news? You're leaving? Like I'm supposed to be surprised or something? I can't remember one three-month stretch in this relationship when you didn't have one foot out the door. So, what is it this time? I'm too distant? Too clingy? Too self-centered, or way too much of a pest, because I'm always trying to do little things for you? Whatever it is, in a month or two, you'll forgive me for being wholly inadequate, and wait patiently for me to beg you to come back. And stupid me, I'll do it. Don't ask me why…

19.

Oh, come on. Admit it. Don't you get that little extra thrill when some stranger smiles at you for no reason at all? When your eyes meet, and they don't look away. When they let you know... with just their eyes...that they find you interesting. Maybe even attractive. We all need to feel wanted now and then. You get caught up in a relationship where you slowly begin to take each other for granted. The excitement slips away, and before you know it, you've become almost invisible... or worse, a constant source of annoyance. A constant source of annoyance to someone who swore they would love you forever... Anyway, a little harmless flirtation never hurt anyone. Don't you think?

20.

Can you hear that? That's my heart pounding. It happens every time I get ready to audition. Part of me doesn't think I'm ready. And the rest says this role was made for me. That I'm going to crush it. Dazzle them with how perfect I am. Well, maybe not perfect. But good enough to do this. Good enough to sparkle. To make this part my own. Now – Deep breath – push the jitters way down in my chest. Chin up. Eyes confident. Relaxed smile firmly in place. This is my time. My moment. This is what I was born to do. And I am ready. I really am. All they have to do is see it! Here I go. Wish me luck!

21.

God, I love this. The heat. The smoke. The smell. The chaos. People crying and screaming like it's them getting burned up, instead of all their trash and memories. Me and my buddies all suited up and running straight into the firestorm, dodging flaming chunks of ceiling as they crash down around us. And on a good day, spotting some scared-to-death little kid that got left behind in the panic. Seeing him, wide-eyed and shivering, crouched in some dark corner as his entire world explodes right in front of him. Talking that little guy back to sanity long enough to throw him over my shoulder and run right through those life-sucking flames to the safety of his terrified and grateful momma's arms. That's the moment every fireman lives for. Hear what I'm sayin'?

22.

I want to be bad. Not just think about it, like I've been doing all my life. I want to do it. I want to forget every rule and every commandment that's been droned into my head since I was little. I want to walk straight up to the first good-looking stranger I find and say, "Take me." To lose myself in unfamiliar arms, making promises I never intend to keep, to someone who'll never even know my name. Just for one night, I don't want to be good or responsible or…or me. Just for one night, and one night only, I want to be free from the burden of being me. Is that so much to ask?

23.

It's gone. All gone. Our savings. Our retirement money. Everything. I lost it all. I was so sure about Chuck's investment advice. I mean, he's my brother, so I knew he wouldn't steer me wrong. He kept telling me it was a sure thing. An inside tip on a stock that was about to blow up. Couldn't fail. Said he was even putting in his own money in. And he pushed me hard. Called me a wimp for not taking risks. Said that's the kind of person that lets down his family. So, I gave him everything. The 401k. The kid's college money. I even took another loan against the house. I know I should have told you, but he said not to. I should just surprise you with a trip around the world when the big payoff hit. That first week, he sent over a bottle of champagne, saying we'd all be millionaires in six months. Two weeks later, he said it may take a little longer… I should have known something was up when he stopped returning my calls. After the news broke, I went to his house to ask him if the charges were true. He just looked at me with that smirk on his face, then slammed the door on me. I begged him to talk to me. Just explain what happened. What went wrong. But he wouldn't even talk to me. Not a word. Now I hear he's run off to somewhere in the Caribbean, living on a yacht, and using what's left of our money to hire lawyers to fight the charges. So, I lost it all. There's nothing left. And I am so…so very sorry.

24.

Don't try to keep up with me. Your little minds can't handle it. See, when you think at warp speed and the rest of the world is stumbling along at a month beyond Neanderthal...well, it's almost sad. I pity them, I really do. I pity their tiny little minds, totally preoccupied with their feeble little problems. As if it really matters whether some schools overly-glandular students carry an inflated animal carcass a few more feet down a grass field than some other schools overly- glandular students? Or whether their silly paper-pushing bosses will let them off an hour early from some meaningless jobs, that only matter to them and no one else.
But I guess that's the only benefit of not being me. You're too stupid to realize how insignificant your lives really are.

25.

I'm sorry. It was me. I did it, and I shouldn't have. I don't even know why I did it. I messed up. I just didn't think. What can I say? Maybe I just wanted to see how you'd react. Maybe I just did it to see if you'd notice I was alive. Maybe I'm tired of being invisible, while you seem to notice everyone else in the world, except me. That's no excuse, I know. I'm not proud of what I did. And I'm not trying to blame you. But it wouldn't hurt if you noticed that I have feelings, too. You know?

26.

I'm not sure, but I don't believe you can truly hate someone until you marry them. It sounds strange, I know, but it's true. You start out all eager and excited, with your heart wide open and a twenty-four-hour dopey grin on your face, that refuses to go away. You love staring into each other's eyes, the warm softness of each other's touch, and all the silly things you do to make each other's laugh like little kids again. You get all jumbled up in forever, and happiness and instant memories that'll last a lifetime... And then the door slams shut. Everything that felt so right is suddenly too uncomfortable to bear. The warm soft touch turns icy. The look in their eyes grows cold and accusing. The silly things they used to say become screams and complaints of how you never do enough. How you're never good enough. Forever begins to feel like a death sentence, and all those wonderful memories are crowded out by petty scorekeeping…who was the last one to take the garbage out? And who left that dirty glass in the sink? No, you can never really hate someone until you marry them. Because when you do, you give them permission to hurt you like no one else ever could. You give them all your hopes and your dreams and your future…then watch them pick it all apart. You hate them for the endless pain they caused you, and for making you feel like such a fool. And you hate yourself for doing the exact same thing to them, every single day...

27.

Tell me about yourself. Tell me everything. I want to know every detail of your life. What makes you happy? What makes you sad? What makes you like me?

I mean, you could be with anyone you wanted. Anybody in the world. But you're here right now...with me...and I find that absolutely amazing.

So, come on. Tell me everything. I want to know.

28.

There they sit...Watching me. Three judges, so tired because they think they've seen it all. But they haven't seen *me* yet. They haven't seen my heart...my dreams... my potential. They're looking up at me and thinking... "It's just another kid who wants to be the next big thing." So how do I make them see I'm so much more than that? I've got sixty seconds to let them know I can do it all. Sing, dance, act.

I'm not after the fame. I'm not looking for a hand out here. I just need one chance. Just one chance to put it all out there and take my shot.

It's like in that musical Cabaret, when that Sally Bowles character sings... *"Maybe this time, I'll win!* Maybe this time... If I can just convince them that I'm something more than Contestant Number 273. I'm Gracie Harcourt. And I know I have what it takes to be a star. I only hope those judges can see that...

29.

There are times I really don't know who I am. Not like I forget my name or anything…I just amaze myself with how shallow I can be. They wanted me there. They needed me to take part. And I was there, like everyone expected me to be. The good friend. The shoulder to cry on. That's me. But all I could think to myself was, who are these people? What do they really mean to my life? Do I even care what they're going through? If not, what kind of cold-hearted hypocrite am I? Of course, I didn't say any of that to them. I continued to listen and nod some more. Even squeezed out a few tears, though I don't know where they came from. The face of compassion. Or that's what they thought. Because they couldn't see what I'm really like. Couldn't see through the mask. Sometimes I don't really know myself at all…

30.

We both know I shouldn't, but I want you to hold me. I need to feel your arms wrapped all around me, and your warm breath whispering soft kisses on my cheek. I want to disappear inside your gentle eyes. Melt into your comforting smile. And feel your heart pounding hard inside my own chest. I want that moment to never end. Because this is where I belong. Here, alone with you. Nobody else in the world. Just you and me, and this endless aching hunger. So please, hold me like you'll never let me go. And then just walk away, and don't look back. I couldn't take it if you looked back.

31.

I used to do this for a living. I know that's hard to
believe, but it's true. I was really good at it. I made a
name for myself. People in the field looked up to me,
because I was the best. Until the stroke, that is. That
damn stroke changed everything. They once said I had a
gift. That these hands were magic, the way they could
take a piece of cold, lifeless stone and tenderly work it
into something beautiful...something unique. Something
that became eloquent and alive just because I touched it.
I soothed it. I transformed it with these hands. With
these hands... I had a gift, then I had a stroke. And just
like that, the gift was gone. The name meant nothing.
And these hands turned more cold and lifeless than the
stone I used to work on. Let me give you a piece of
advice... Don't ever define yourself by what you do.
Because if you ever lose it... If that passion, that gift is
ever taken away from you...then you lose all sense of
who you are. You only remember what you lost...

32.

Have you noticed that our conversations no longer start
with "Where are you from?" Now the first thing we ask
is "What do you do?" As neighborhoods and personal
identities fade, our careers are all that's left to define us.
We are no longer home or history. We are nothing more
than walking resumes, as if only our job can tell the
world who we really are. How sad is that?

33.

Toughen up, kid. This is life. Real life. Accidents happen. Nations go to war. And you and I come home to find your Mom passed out in her own vomit again. Now you can either cry about it, let it twist and tear at your insides, until one day you wake to find you're as much a pill poppin' pantywaist as she is… or you can soldier up and tell yourself this kind of thing will NOT define you. This will NOT ruin your life. This will NOT be the childhood memory you pass along to your own kids somewhere down the line… Now you just wipe those tears away, and go brush your teeth, while I go clean up your Mother. I'll be upstairs in twenty to read you a bedtime story. And hey, Mister…don't you ever forget that you are precious to me. And that I love you more than life itself… Now scat, little man! You and I got a job to do! I'm proud of you, soldier…

34.

See this? This is me ignoring you. This is me not listening to any of your excuses. To any of your lies. This is me not being wrapped around your finger anymore. Forced to play desperate puppy to your non-stop, every day, twenty-four-hour princess act. This me deciding I deserve better. This is me not caring anymore.
And in case you still don't get it…this is me leaving. Even if most of me doesn't want to…

35.

You're right. I still don't know what I'm going to do with my life. Have no idea at all. There are so many things I want to do, but like you always told me… maybe I'm not smart enough, or talented enough, or even want it bad enough to make it. So, no, Dad. I don't know what I want or what I'm going to do. I just know what I *don't* want…and that's your life. The life you expect me to live. With all the restrictions and fears and boundaries and pretenses that have warped and crippled you so badly, you can't even see how unhappy you really are. And maybe I'll be unhappy too. Maybe I'll be the failure you always knew I'd be. But at least I'll have done something different. At least I'll have tried to live. Tried to live my way. And maybe that'll be enough.

36.

Sometimes, the kindest thing you can do is walk away. When nothing you say or do comes out right, and everything has to be reinterpreted to cover up the pain and resentment that builds just being in the same room together. You try to be polite, or at least civil to each other, because that's what everybody says we're supposed to be. I know you don't want to hurt me, or at least, you don't want me to suffer all that much. But I can see in your eyes that you're waiting for that speeding bus, or trip on the stairs, or random piece of food to stick in my throat to set you free. And the worst part is…I'm so desperately hoping for the same thing.

37.

How can you be so…perfect? You have those big dark eyes that always look so sad and beautiful. Like some Renaissance painting, only softer, kinder. And your lips, so full and tempting, and mischievous. That's it. You have mischievous lips. The kind that pull in just a little, like you want to laugh, only you won't let yourself. And when you finally do, that smile of yours melts me. Melts me down to the core. Like nothing in the world can make me as happy as making you happy. And the funny thing is, you don't even realize how amazingly perfect you really are. You don't know how much faster I start breathing when I see you, or how I have to look away before anyone notices me staring at your face. You have no idea what you do to me, just by being in the same room. And that makes it even more perfect, you know?

38.

I can do this. I know I can do this. I don't care how scared I am, or how many people are watching. I know I can do this. It's strange how the more you want something, the harder it is to stand up and grab it. I don't know why. Maybe I don't want to disappoint them. Don't want them to see me fail. But that's just the fear talking. And fear is a lie. A silly little whisper keeping me from what I really want. And what I want is to do this. To show them what I'm made of. Show them how special I am. I can do this. I know I can. Just watch me!

39.

Listen up. And you better listen up good. There's more than one enemy out there, and the baddest one ain't carrying no weapon you can see. Your worst enemy by far is fear. That's right, fear. You give in to it, and you're dead without even knowin' it. When you're in country, fear is like sharp pieces of broken glass. You can look right through it, and it ain't nothin' special. But you swallow that fear…take it internally, and those sharp edges are gonna cut your guts up somethin' fierce. Swallow enough of it, and it'll flat out kill you. You hear me? Now we got us a job to do, and it sure as hell ain't gonna be easy. But you just leave all your fear lyin' there on the ground. Crush it with your boot, if you have to, and soldier on. You got that? Good. Now let's move out.

40.

You don't have to worry about me. In fact, I'd rather you didn't think of me at all. Because after all these years, after all we've been through, I won't be thinking about you at all. I don't intend to waste one more minute on your fantasies, your pitiful excuses, or the mess you made out of both our lives. You can be sure that if you ever do cross my mind, you'll be like one of those framed photos in a museum. Nothing but a frozen, lifeless image of the past. Safely hidden behind a cold piece of glass. Some memories are better that way, and you're one of them. Trust me, I've got better things to think about than you.

41.

Tomorrow they are putting me in a nursing home.
Tonight, we're having chicken.
Somehow an entire life of laughter, joy and fear has
slipped right past me, marked only by a series of memories
too elusive to hold in my swollen hands, too desperately
painful to let go of.
I never knew I could get this old... I never knew I could
feel this... frightened. I fought every obstacle to build a life
for me and my family. But suddenly, somehow, I became
too old to fight. Too tired to make the choices. Too lonely
to live out my life without someone to need me. My own
children...old enough to know the pain I'm feeling...are
sitting around the table trying to pretend that tomorrow
is just another day. But we all know it isn't...
This is the saddest chicken I have ever tasted...

42.

Don't worry. You are not a disappointment to me.
To be disappointed, I'd have to have expected more
from you. I would have to believe that you could have
done better. But we both learned a long time ago, that
was never going to happen. That no matter what, you
would find some immature and irresponsible way to let
everyone down. To embarrass yourself. And us...
So, no, I am not disappointed with you.
Just sad that you always manage to live down to my
expectations.

43.

Okay, let's be straight here. You don't like me and I sure as hell don't like you. You see me as two steps below roadkill, and as far as I'm concerned, you could cough up a lung and start hemorrhaging right here in front of me, and I wouldn't lift a finger to clean up the mess. But we have one thing in common, and that's our kids. They didn't clear it with us before they became best friends, or I would have said no freakin' way. But they get along, and that's what we're left with. I'd do anything for my daughter, even if that means not gutting you on sight. So as long as our kids are best friends, you and I'll just have to pretend we can stand the sight of each other. Deal?

44.

I can hear them. I can hear them out there. Waiting. Waiting until I'm not paying attention. When they think I'm distracted, or not ready to fight them off the moment they come for me.
They think they can sneak up on me and smother me in my sleep. But I'm always ready. Even if it means I never leave this room. Even if it means I never sleep. Even if it means I never do anything but sit here, staring at the door and window with this shotgun in my hand.
They think they're so smart, but I'm smarter.
And I can hear them.
Waiting… Just waiting…

45.

I love days like this. Laying out in the sun. Feeling that soft, velvety warmth melt away all the tension and worries of the day. You there beside me. Looking like you have always been here. Always belonged in a place like this. Always belonged with me.

It doesn't really matter what we talk about. Silly stuff, deep philosophy, or the thousand things people do that piss you off. We're here in paradise. No problems to solve. Nothing to accomplish. Just you and me enjoying this place, the weather, and each other.

I desperately want to remember this moment. When it feels like my world is everything it was meant it to be.

46.

I don't get it. You're not my type. We have nothing in common. I'm pretty sure you don't even really like me. And any other day, I wouldn't have given you a second look. So, tell me why it is that I can't get you out of my mind? And why, when I'm with you, do I feel more comfortable and happier than I have for years? How is it that I can always know what you're thinking, and how you are able to finish my sentences before I even get my words out? Look, we both know this is never going to work. We have no future together. I don't see us ever being an 'us.' But damn if I can get through a single day without thinking of your smile. Your eyes. Your crazy way of looking at things. The way you make me feel... I don't know. I don't get it. I don't get it at all.

47.

I watched you disappear last week. You were sitting at
the kitchen table, drinking your coffee and talking about
the usual frustrations of your day, in all that excruciating
detail. Then suddenly, you just… disappeared. Your body
was still there. Even your voice droned on. But listening
to you spout another one of your endless, lifeless litanies
of complaint, trying to pass that off as conversation…
you suddenly disappeared out of my life. The person I
fell in love with so many years ago was gone. Vanished
right before my eyes. And all that was left was this angry,
empty shadow of you at the table. Droning on and on.
Until I finally had to leave the room and cry.

48.

All my life, people have been talking about 'my potential.'
My potential…like it's some kind of massive mystical
thing I've gotta serve. "You're so talented. You've got so
much potential"… "I wish had half as much potential as
you!"… "You're not living up to your potential, kid!"
You know what potential really is? It's this great weight
that other people put on you. Live up to your potential
or you're letting everyone down. Letting yourself down.
But nobody ever tells you exactly *how* to live up to your
potential. And if you somehow manage to, don't they just
lay on even more potential you have to live up to?
So, what's the point? Huh?

49.

It's close. So close, I can almost taste it. I've been so focused for so long, and now it's all about to happen for me. After all that work and sacrifice and dedication, I know I'm gonna make it. Gonna make it big. All my dreams are about to become reality. This time next year, I'll have it all. The big house. The name in lights. The freedom to do what I want, whenever I want. It's been a long, hard road, but I'm almost there. Really. I can feel it.

50.

I had this dream the other night. I was lost and alone in some strange part of town. Something was after me, but I didn't know what. It was all shadows and night, and I could feel this intense cold, like the icy hand of death squeezing my spine. I was running through these dark, maze-like alleys that fed into each other, pulling me deeper and deeper inside. I ran with slow, dead legs, screaming as hard as I could, but no sound came out. And then, suddenly…I felt your gentle breath on my neck. Your arm slipped across my chest, and your body cuddled up next to mine. I'm not even sure you were awake when you whispered in my ear "It's all right. It's all right." And then your breath slowed and softened, your body still wrapped around me like another layer of warm, smooth skin.
And that's what I love about you. Awake or asleep, you always know what I need.

51.

Wow… I never thought I'd be here. Starting over. All alone at this stage of my life. It seemed it took forever to find that one person I could finally talk to. Someone who really 'got' me. Who understood and didn't judge me at all. Someone I could cherish, and love, and even be silly with. Someone who would cherish and love me in return. My soulmate. The person I wanted to spend the rest of my life with. You know, for the longest time, I was afraid that person didn't exist. But then you walked into my life, and suddenly everything was…I don't know… perfect. But hey, I guess nothing good lasts forever. Love fades. Dreams die. Recriminations pile up. And maybe once you looked deep enough, you didn't really like what you saw. You realized I wasn't enough for you. So, I guess it's time for me to start over, and hope there's at least one more person out there willing to take a chance on me. Maybe even love me, like you did once. But enough of that... Where do I sign?

52.

You think you're such a mystery, but you're not. I can see you coming from miles away. I know what you're thinking. I know what you're feeling. I know what you want and what you're afraid of. Oh, yeah. I know *exactly* what you're afraid of. You're as transparent as glass to me. And believe me…I know a million different ways to crush you. You wait and see...

53.

They took my baby away. Just came right in and took
him. I swore I'd never let them do that again. Not after
the last two. They don't have the right! Sure, I get mad
sometimes. Who doesn't? They just don't know what it's
like around here. I'm under a lot of pressure, y'know?
And those kids don't help none by runnin' around and
screamin' all the time. I mean, I know they're hungry, but
they don't have to scream about it. And just because I get
mad now and then and swat their butts when they push
me to far, it don't make me no bad parent. Kids are…
what's that word? Resilient. Yeah, resilient. They bounce
back. And I'm just doin' what my Daddy taught me. I
took my share of whacks when I pushed him too far.
And I didn't turn out all that bad. No, sir. I'm just doin'
my job as a parent. And besides, it's not my fault if Troy
Junior bruises easier than most kids. They got no right to
keep taking my babies away from me. I'm a parent. I got
rights. I got rights.

54.

I'm sorry. I can't imagine the pain you're going through.
How terrible that must feel. It just breaks my heart to see
you like this. You deserve so much better.
But I want you to remember…I'll be there for you if you
ever need me.
That's what friends are for.

55.

He's lying to me. I can tell. I can always tell. Oh, he
thinks he's doing everything right. Nodding and
gesturing at the right moments. Leaning closer, as if his
words were a soft intimacy meant only for me. That
overly sincere smile. The thoughtful pauses. But there's
something about his eyes as he speaks. A coldness. And
an occasional flicker, like a fear of getting caught. He's
trying way too hard to not look away while he explains
where all the money went, or why he had to work so late
at the office every night this week. He's gotten much
better at lying to me, but I can still tell. And all the time
he's lying to my face, I nod and smile in sympathetic
understanding. I tell him I believe him. I tell him, and he
relaxes. He thinks he's safe. Thinks he's won. And he
believes me, because unlike him, my eyes never give away
what I really feel inside. What I'm up to. All the things he
will never know. You see, the truth is I'm a much better
liar than he will ever be. And I despise him for it.

56.

You don't understand. It's not the money that bothers
me. It's not even losing it, or the fact that I managed to
mess up yet again. I can always find a way to turn a sure
thing, or easy answer into another pile of dog crap. I'm
used to it. But what I can't take is looking foolish. I know
I'm a loser and an idiot and the world's biggest screw up.
But, dear God, how I hate being ridiculous. And that
look of pity in your eyes only makes it worse…

57.

Yeah, that's my mom over there. The smiley blonde bragging about me to all the other parents. She does that all the time. It is so like, totally cringe-y. But moms are like that, I guess. I know we don't look alike, because she's not my biological mother. I don't remember much about my bio-mom, except that she dumped me in a shopping cart in the produce section when I was two. Turned around and never came back. I guess I was crying for a while when my mom – this mom – noticed a little baby all alone and called the store manager, who called the police, who called child protective services, who finally came and took me away. But this mom – the smiley blonde one - kept calling to see if I was all right. When they couldn't find the woman who abandoned me, this mom asked to adopt me. She fought for me, even though she had six kids of her own. So yeah, that's my mom. My real mom. And always will be.

58.

That's it. I'm empty. Running on fumes. I don't know why, but everything I am, everything I hoped and felt, everything I loved has drained right out of me. Until I'm left like this. Just a cold, withered shell with my face on it. Floating disconnected through a life that used to be real. Used to be mine. I feel like any second a strong wind could grab this dried husk, and I'd crumble into ash and disappear. Just blow away without a trace... And I wonder. Would anyone notice? Would anyone care at all?

59.

You know me. I never make promises. I've known too many people in this world who make promises they can't keep. Or never intended to in the first place. And I swore to myself a long time ago, I would never be like that. If I give my word, I mean it. So, when we got engaged and I promised to love you forever, I meant it. When we stood at that altar, and both swore eternal love, that was real. That was forever... But yesterday, I found another set of bruises on Allie's back. I know she can be a handful, but she's four. Only four years old. She's still learning about right and wrong. But you, you're an adult. You should know better. Now I know I promised to love you forever. But when I see Allie wince every time you hug her. And cower in that corner whenever you walk in the room. Well, that's my baby girl. So as far as I'm concerned, forever ends today.

60.

I like you. I like the look of your face. The way your eyes see right through me. Reach deep into my soul. I know we've never met. Well, not yet anyway. But you have such power over me. The way your picture looks at me from the computer screen pins me to my chair. Sometimes for hours. Sometimes for whole days. And when I asked you to be my friend on Facebook, you agreed. Like we were meant for each other. Like this was meant to be. You just don't know it yet...

61.

This ain't no kind of life. No kind of life at all. A body ain't s'posed to hurt this much. Knees all shot to hell and my right hip screamin' at me all night long. I go to bed tired and sore and wake up next day twice as bad. Head poundin' and stomach all tied up in knots. If I'm lucky, I'll get three, maybe four hours a night. That's why I need 'em. The Oxy, the Codeine and the Demerol. Nothin' else gets me through the day. So, don't you go lecturin' me 'bout them pills. You don't feel what I feel. You don't suffer, day in and day out like I do. I need 'em. They get me through. An' I just want the pain to go away, is all. Just want the pain to go away.

62.

Tell me, what can I do to make you happy? The way you used to be. Like you were when we first met. That's what attracted to me to you in the first place. You were this bright yellow light of joy, bubbling with laughter over everything you saw. Like the way a child first sees the world. You had this contagious happiness that seemed to spill onto everyone around you, everyone you touched. It was so wonderful, so irresistible. But that light is gone. Vanished, along with the laughter. And I don't know what I did to kill it so completely. I always gave you whatever you wanted, and still you sit there with that look of total boredom and contempt on your face. So please, tell me what I can do to make you happy again?

63.

Thank you for coming in, Stanley. Please, have a seat...
Now I know you have only worked here thirteen
months, and sometimes it does take a little while to get
used to a new company and their policies.
So maybe you didn't know that the workday begins at
9 AM, and not 9:45 or 10:20, depending on traffic.
Or that your lunch hour is actually only an hour long.
And it's probably my fault for not posting our firm's
sexual harassment policy in 78-point type, so you would
realize how inappropriate it is to offer free massages to
every female employee who steps into the break
room…which you evidently confuse with your office,
since you seem to spend the majority of your day there.
And perhaps the Employee Manual wasn't exactly clear
about taking home office supplies, browsing porn sites
on your office computer, or telling our customers that
the company president is a…how did you put it…? 'A
cash-grubbing moron with all the charm and class of a
dead salamander.'
So, since the communication problem appears to be
mine, let me try to make this simple...
You're fired.
I hope that's clear enough?

64.

I think about it sometimes... No, that's a lie. I think about it all the time. It barges into my head when I hear you on the phone. It whispers in my ear at night, when I'm pretending to sleep. Even when I try hard not to, I think about it. Those two terrible little words. The most destructive and seductive words in the English language...What if? What if we weren't together? What if I never met you? What if I had the guts to leave you right now, and finally stand on my own two feet? What if...? And then I realize, it's never gonna happen. We're stuck in this, you and me. Trapped somewhere between boredom and contempt. Trying desperately to get though each day without killing each other. Or wanting to kill ourselves. What if it wasn't like this?

I just wish I had the courage to find out...

65.

There's a place beyond emptiness... I know. I've been there. It's a dark, cold world filled only by the ghosts of regret and the harsh, rasping sound of unspoken words, broken promises and things you wish you had done, but could never find the time for. I...I didn't always live here. I once felt at home in the real world. At home with you. But when you left me, there was nowhere else I fit in. No place I belonged anymore.

Except here...alone...

In that place beyond emptiness.

66.

I want to say something, but I don't want to spoil the moment. I spend too much of my days talking, babbling about my feelings, and bludgeoning everyone with my 'important' views and insights. But now, holding you like this, your head resting on my shoulder, the warm kiss of your breath on my chest, the absolute, soul-soothing peace of being alone with you. Suddenly, there's nothing left to say. No words to capture how right it feels with you in my arms. How precious this tender blanket of shared silence is to me. 'I love you' doesn't do it justice. 'I need you' is clingy and inadequate. 'I pray this never ends' is too obvious. So, I'll keep my exploding thoughts to myself, and concentrate on the soft whisper of your breath… as our hearts slowly learn to beat as one.

67.

I know what heaven is. At least what I know what it is for me. Heaven is where you can finally be free of all the foolish mistakes and life-numbing decisions of your past. Without all the crippling obligations that grind away on your soul, day after day. Where the infinite possibilities of childhood live again. Free to follow anywhere your heart leads. Never worrying who you're disappointing, or whose definition of responsibility you are not living up to. Heaven is the one place I can drink in your eyes, kiss your hair, and lose myself in your smile, without having to worry about our feeble chances at a future, or my own suffocating past. At least that's what heaven is to me…

68.

Listen. You and me go way back. We've known each
other since Seventh Grade. You were in my wedding,
and I was in yours. Our kids play together. We've shared
vacations and holidays and birthdays and funerals
together. But, man, I am so tired of arguing with you.
We just don't think the same way about politics these
days. And we probably never will again. But that don't
mean we have to fight all the time. It don't mean I'm
stupid, or a terrible person just because you don't like
who I voted for. And I can't understand how in hell you
can vote for your candidate either.
So why can't we agree to disagree without absolutely
hating each other, or calling each other names, okay?
Four years from now, there'll be another election and we
can argue then. But for now, let's just remember that
we're friends. What do you say?

69.

Shhh. Come here. I've got to tell you something...
You've got to promise you won't tell anybody. It'll just
be our little secret. The truth is…I wrote the letter. I
know everyone thinks it was him, but it was me. I didn't
mean to cause all that trouble, but…well, I'm not sorry I
wrote it. And I don't know. Maybe I'd do it all over again
if I had to… Just promise you won't tell anyone else.
It'll be our little secret.

70.

I heard you. I'm depressed. Excuse me, 'Clinically Depressed.' Poor me. I mean look at the news. Every day, millions of people are dying of starvation, or being shot or blown up by psychotic idiots. They're alone, out in the cold, feeling their bodies waste away from disease. They've seen parents and children and pieces of their own bodies ripped away in accidents or violence. They've lost everything they had, or never had anything to begin with. They are broke, starving, terrified that any second could be filled with mind-shattering agony. And me? I feel unhappy that I didn't get all the pats on the back I think I deserve. The way I see it, if you're awake in this world, you're suffering. Depression is the natural reaction to life's random, unending cruelty. So, you tell me to take these meds to make everything better? I guess the hundred thousand tortured souls gasping their painful, frightened last breaths must be feeling sorry for me having to swallow these expensive chemicals, just so I won't feel so bad today. Like I said, poor me.

71.

Look, I'm doing the best I can here! I don't know what you expect of me. Ever since I met you, you've been looking at me like I don't measure up. Like I'm not good enough, or something. I tried everything. I just don't know what else to do. What is it you want me to do, huh? Should I just go? Is that what you want?

72.

It has taken me all these years to realize memories don't live in the mind. They live in your eyes, your ears, your hands, and your heart. When I close my eyes, I can still see her twirling around in that little princess dress; her shiny black shoes, white gloves and carefully tied ponytail speckled with sunlight. In those dreamy velvet moments before I wake, I hear her tiny laugh tickling my ears, and relive the warm, sad feeling of that precious little hand in mine. The way those little fingers squeezed tight when she was scared, and even tighter when she was giggly with happiness.

Even now, my chest fills with my own giggly loneliness every time I think of those little arms reaching out to me for comfort, or the simple joy of having daddy walk through the door. And my heart still beats tighter when I remember how her eyes sparkled with delight in the shadowy softness of a new bedtime story.

She's gone now. Building a life that doesn't require grown-up hands, a parent's hugs, or daddy's stories.

She calls or drops me an email now and then, and I guess that's the way it's supposed to be.

But here I am on the back side of life, with nothing left to hold onto but this lonely tingling in my empty hand, the echo of little girl whispers…

And a huge, memory-filled chasm in the heart of a father left behind much too soon.

73.

It's almost more than I can take. Sometimes, I can't even believe this is happening to me. I mean you are so... so...perfect. Every night, I lay there in the dark, listening to your soft breath. Looking at your face as you sleep. Thinking to myself, how did I get so lucky? What the hell did I ever do to be so blessed? I know time drains the wonder from our eyes and grinds away at every feeling. And I know that someday, I may take it all for granted. We'll be like every other old married couple. I'll wake up, yawn, and stumble into the shower, not even bothering to look at the angel sleeping softly in my bed. Forgive me for that day. Don't let it come too soon. Because I don't want to lose this desperate, tearing hold you have over my heart. Even though it's almost more than I can take.

74.

Anyone can look at the downside of life. Get depressed. Let all the pain and aggravation build up 'til you want to scream at anyone that gets in your way. And who could blame you? But that's the easy way out. A strong person, a person of character, goes through all that and still tries to force out a smile. Now I know people think I'm some kind of silly fool, and maybe they're right. But I know what it takes to look at the good side when your entire world is falling apart. It takes faith and gratitude. Thanking heaven above that you made it through another day, no matter what that day turns out to be. So as long as I'm able to choose, I choose to be cheerful.

75.

I've been cheated in my marriage. That's right, cheated. It's not like my wife had an affair or anything. That would have been easier to deal with... No, I feel cheated because she isn't the person I thought I was getting when we married. She used to be so...so confident and fun and alive. I couldn't help but feel this was the person I'd been searching for all my life. A partner who could inspire me. To work beside me on whatever crazy idea popped into our heads. Everything was exciting. Everything seemed possible. Together, we could accomplish anything. But that was a long time ago. Some may call it settling, but it's not. It's more like...realizing. Realizing that the person you thought you were marrying was a fiction. A fairy tale. A lie. And there are no 'truth in advertising' laws in marriage...

76.

Stop telling me what to do. I'm not a child anymore. I don't need someone telling me what I can or can't do. Who I can be friends with. What I'm allowed to spend my money on. And even what I'm supposed to think. I don't need a boss or a dictator. I don't need someone to throw me down or remind me that I'm a total disappointment. You think I don't know that already? You think you haven't made that clear? You think you don't say it in a million different ways? I'm not a child. And I'm not going to let you treat me like one anymore. If you can't handle that...then get out of my life.

77.

It's okay. I know you're tired. But you can rest now. We both know you've earned it. You've done your job. You've worked hard. Protected us all these years. You've got so much to be proud of. A nice house. A good name. A beautiful family. And more children and grandchildren than we ever thought we'd live to see. They all love you and they're all so proud of you.

So, you've done your job. You can rest now. You've done so much for all of us. It's time to rest now. Just close your eyes and go to sleep. It'll be all right.

I promise I will miss you every day of my life... But I'll get through it.

So, you can sleep now. Just go to sleep...

78.

Surprise me. That's all I want. Just surprise me. Do something that is so... I don't know...so completely out of character that I'll be knocked right out of my chair. Like maybe saying something nice to me, when you don't want or expect anything in return. Or giving me just one compliment, or even a simple 'thank you' to show you recognize all the crap I do for you around here. Or how about noticing that I even exist when you walk into the house? Give me a nod before you go close your door and lock me out of whatever you're doing in that room...

As I said...surprise me.

79.

She didn't call for Christmas again this year. My own daughter didn't even call me for Christmas. Or New Years. Or Valentine's Day, or even my birthday. No call. No gift. No card. Not even a text message. I send her gifts. I call, and she never picks up. Every call goes straight to voicemail and are never get returned. I don't understand it. She wasn't raised like this. I gave her everything she wanted and told her each and every day how much she was loved, and that I was always proud of her. So, what happened to her? Was I that terrible a parent? Was I that horrible a person? Please tell me what exactly did I do to be so - not hated - but ignored? And what do I do now?

80.

You disgust me. I can't even look at you anymore. You play like you're a saint, this martyr who is constantly suffering for others. But it's a lie. Everything about you is a lie. You're the most selfish person I know. You only care about others if you can get something from them. They're nothing more than emotional ATMs to you. You push their buttons and take out whatever you want. Pity, connections or cash, anything that serves your needs. You're nothing but a liar and a user. It took me so long to figure out, but that's all you are. You may have everybody else fooled, but not me. I see who you are. I know what you're really like. And you disgust me…

81.

Send me up through the sky. Let me dance among the planets and asteroids. It's been so long since I felt the sheer wonder of a child. Give me something that'll rattle my imagination until I gasp with amazement.

Being an astronaut is part scientist, part adventurer and part seeker of truth and enlightenment. I want to find my feet a million miles above solid ground. I want to look back at the place of my birth and see that glowing blue jewel hanging in all that black nothingness, calling me home, and encouraging me to explore and experience things only a handful of humans have ever seen.

So, NASA, here I come. Hey, solar system, I'm moving in. Mars, get ready for your new roommate!

Three, two, one...let the adventure begin!

82.

The bus is here. I'm going now. I'm sorry, it's time. But I want you to know...It's important you realize... What I'm trying to say is...just, well...thank you. Thank you for all you've done for me. Thank you for being so sweet and supportive, even when you didn't agree with my choices. And for loving me, even when I wasn't able to love myself. You made me stronger. You made me whole. And I just wanted to say thank you for that. Thank you so much...

83.

It ain't so bad. Dyin'. It ain't anywhere near as bad as
people think. You just feel yourself slippin' away, bit by
bit. All those things you used to do without thinkin',
things like breathin' and swallowin' or even getting' out
of this damn bed and goin' to the bathroom under your
own power...little by little, you lose all that. But the
kindness of it is that you start to forget what it was like
before. Before everything from your eyes to your kidneys
stopped working right. Before your legs gave up on you.
Before you were trussed up in this all-consumin' teeth-
grindin' agony. And as the days drag on, it gets to seem
like it was always this way. You was always dyin'. You
was just somehow too busy to notice. And then you get
to the point where it just seems like the right thing to do.
Passin' away. Lettin' all those foolish cares and 'shoulda
dones' pass before your eyes and fritter away. No more
worries. No more pain. No more indignity. No more
me... So, it ain't so bad, this dyin' thing. You just gotta
look at it the right way...

84.

Nobody really sees you. At least they don't see me.... It's
not like I'm invisible or anything. I just seem to fade into
the background. I walk down the street and people look
right through me, as if I'm not even there. But I am here.
I really am! I have thoughts and hopes and dreams. And
one day, the world will see just how special I really am.

85.

I'm glad you came. There's no easy way to tell you this. The tests came back and I'm sorry to say, it doesn't look good. Your mother has Alzheimer's. And it's already reached the intermediate to advanced stages. Fortunately, she's not really aware of what's happening to her. She seems to be reliving something from when she was much younger. Something about a picnic back in Minnesota when she was a teenager. She seems happy there, which is good. Not everyone reverts to happy memories. But don't be surprised if she doesn't recognize you. She may have only sporadic access to memories after the age of fifteen. She may not remember ever being married, or even having children. You can't take it personally. It's the nature of the disease. And it will only get worse. Your job is to comfort her. No matter how confused she gets, remember that somewhere deep inside, there may be a spark of the mother who loved and cared for you.
Now it's your time to care for her.
So, are you ready to see her now?

86.

My parents don't understand what I'm going through. They don't see all the pressure I'm under... Homework. School. Friends. Having to pretend to be someone I'm not just to fit in. And I'm afraid to tell them what I think. What I really feel.
It's like nobody knows me at all.

87.

Okay. I'm on in five minutes. The chance of a lifetime. All my dreams on the line, and only five minutes to prove it. Pressure, pressure, pressure. But I can handle it. I was born to do this. Born to be a star, no matter what anybody says. Okay, so there's a lot of lines. It's a complex part. But I've rehearsed for weeks. I have this down. I *know* this character, inside and out. So, no problem. I've got this. Hollywood, here I come!

88.

I'm an addict. I admit it. I'm not addicted to drugs or booze, or anything. It's you. You're my addiction. Somehow, you crawled inside my skull. Took over my thoughts, my moods, my entire life. I can be having the worst, soul-crushing day, and then I get an email, or little text from you, and suddenly, there I am…smiling like an idiot walking down the street. Everybody's looking at me, like 'what's wrong with him?' I keep your picture on my computer and say, 'Hi there, Beautiful,' a dozen times a day. And when I'm expecting to hear from you, and you don't call or text, I go into complete and utter heartbreak withdrawal. Pacing around the house. Trying to hold on to a thought that doesn't involve your warm eyes, soft touch and knee-weakening smile. Then you finally call, and just like that, everything is perfect with the world again. Because somebody so far out of my league, is crazy enough to love me. So yeah, I'm addicted, and it's all your fault. Just call me, okay?

89.

You killed her. Maybe not with bullets. Maybe not with blood. But you killed her. You killed her with neglect, because you couldn't take your eyes off the insignificant little problems of your own life. You sat back and watched as she pleaded with those enormous, sad eyes. That face, so innocent, so marked by suffering...whose only crime was to be born in a backwards land with brutal politics and a complete lack of humanity for the poorest among them. You watched her on TV like it was a deodorant commercial, and then changed the channel to find something more entertaining. And in those sixty seconds, you gave up an opportunity to rescue a human life for a chance to chuckle over some canned and packaged humor, that you forgot five seconds after you heard it. But don't worry. There are three hundred million more just like her. Children starving and suffering in a hundred desolate countries. Pleading for the smallest morsel, or even a sip of clean water. And just like her, they'll die, while you and I sit back and try desperately to amuse or distract ourselves. May God forgive us.

90.

Hey, whatcha got in the box? is that what I think it is? How'd you get it? I mean, I thought those things were, you know, hard to come by. Do they know you got it? Believe me, I won't say a word. Just let me see it. Just a quick look, okay?

91.

There's nothing worse than watching people in love, when you're the only one who's not. Seeing them laugh at each other's silly jokes. Smile into each other's eyes. Touch each other in that soft, comfortable way. All that going on around you, while you sit there, completely alone, with nobody in the world for you to touch, or laugh with, or even look at. And it's everywhere. I walk down the street and everybody else is holding hands. Go to McDonald's, and everyone is leaning close, feeding each other fries. Movies are the worst, because even superheroes fall in love, and the couple in the seat right next to me are kissing like their lips are glued together, not even watching some douchebag in tights save the planet and win the girl. It's like everyone in the world has found somebody, but me. So, what's wrong with me? Am I that ugly? That unlikeable? And why is it I can't find somebody to love? I really want to know. Why?

92.

I don't deserve this. I don't know why I was singled out like this. I've got a good paying job that I actually enjoy doing. Kids that have never been arrested. Most of my hair and a stable marriage to someone who still thinks I'm sexy after all these years. My life is good, while so many of the people I grew up with are struggling financially, miserable in their marriages or careers, and watching their lives spin out of control.

So why me? Why do I deserve to be so blessed? Why?

93.

I found a couple of photo albums in the dumpster behind my apartment building. Cheap. Blue plastic. The kind you get at the Dollar Store. They were filled with these images of some girl's life. Nothing special, candids of friends. Lots of smiles and memories. Meaningless to anyone, unless you were there. The landlord threw it all out when he was cleaning her apartment. They found her body on the subway last week. I don't even know what she died of. She was only twenty-six. Barely had time to live. They found her, just sitting there in the subway car, riding back and forth, up and down the line. Nobody noticed the motionless girl on the subway for a day and a half. Anyway, I grabbed the photos from the dumpster, because I thought I could use them as notebooks. But when I started to tear out the pictures…something got to me. Here was the last, trivial proof of someone's life…just thrown away. Maybe she didn't have any family. Or maybe nobody cared enough to keep them. Not even the other people in the pictures. This girl was twenty-six years-old and lived in the very same apartment building as me, and I never once said 'hi' to her in the hallway. I didn't even take the time to learn her name. And now that she's gone, I'm haunted by the sheer loneliness of it all. And almost every day, I stare at these old discarded photos. Because someone has to. Someone has to...

94.

Some kids think it's cool to drink. Like getting a buzz on before school or late at night will make you more popular. But don't fall for that... Underage drinking is illegal. It can make you sick or it can take your life. And drinking can also make you do stupid things. You may think everyone is laughing with you, but they're really just laughing at you. So, pass on the drinking, instead of passing out. Because alcohol is no joke.

95.

I'm scared, Mandy. I really am. Not scared of monsters or ghosts or some psycho slasher with a knife sneaking up on me. I'm scared that I'm going to screw up again. Make a mess of my life. Never knowing what I really want to do. Never figuring out what I'm supposed to do. I've seen so many people waste it all. Their time. Their gifts. Their dreams. You see them, decaying from the inside out. Bent over by guilt and regret over all the things they did or didn't do. Until one day they find themselves on the other side of six or seven decades with that same sad, stunned surprise on their wrinkled faces. Like nobody told them it's their time to run, and they missed their chance. Missed it by a mile. And it ain't never coming back around again.
I'm scared, Mandy. I don't want to be one of those people. And I'm afraid I'm halfway there already...

96.

You think this is easy for me? You think I like this? You know how hard it is for me to put a gun to my best friend's head? Do ya? Why you makin' me do this, huh?! Why'd you hafta' go and put me in this situation?! Why couldn't you keep your damn mouth shut? Now I gotta put two in your ear, just to get Eddie the Fig off my back. And then I gotta look at your wife and kids at the funeral, and act like I'm just as torn up about you getting' whacked as they are. You know how tough that's gonna be on me? Don't you ever think about anybody yourself?!

97.

Okay, I tried the forgiveness thing, and it just didn't take. You cheated me, and I let it go, because we were friends. Used to be friends. For that reason, and that reason only, I turned the other cheek and walked away.

But then you had to go and hit me again with your petty little games. As if you are trying so hard to convince the world that you're right and everybody else has to be wrong. So, you stab me in the back again, just because I didn't bow down and kiss your feet. Are you that much of a child? Do you have that much of a god complex that even your friends can't take you aside and whisper a little bit of perspective or constructive criticism?

Well, let me tell you this… you just used your last 'Get To Be A Jerk For Free' card. Forgiveness only goes so far. And you're way, way past that.

98.

It's three AM. Three in the morning, and once again, I'm sitting here in the dark trying to figure out my life. As if my insomnia will grant me some great cosmic insight. Like while I sit here in my underwear, alone in my apartment, listening to the screeching sirens and barely heard screams of a torn-apart city that's supposed to be sleeping…somehow everything will suddenly become clear to me. Somehow, I'll know what to say, what to do, where to go. Either that, or I'll just watch another ten or twelve infomercials, until the sun comes up and it starts all over again.

99.

Is it just me, or was everything so much brighter when we were kids? Colors were more vibrant. Candy tasted sweeter. Do you remember when the crack of a home run hit off a baseball bat sent chills up your spine and pulled screams from your lips? And the smell of homemade cookies made your eyes roll in delight. Nowadays, nothing smells real. Nothing looks alive. I sit in front of a TV all night watching comedies that don't make me laugh and cop shows that don't make me cringe, no matter how many victims pile up. I don't know…Maybe life was meant for kids. Maybe it just fades away - the colors and tastes and smells leaking out without us ever realizing it. Until one day…we do. And all we have left are the memories of a time, long ago, when we were really, truly alive.

100.

You should have seen his smile. It was a smile you couldn't forget. You know how babies' smiles are so infectious? How they seem to laugh with their whole bodies, and you can't help but laugh along with them? That's what Eddie's smile was like. He'd be just sitting there, watching TV, or out with his loser friends, and then he'd turn towards you and flash that sweet, sweet smile, and suddenly, it was okay. Everything felt okay when he smiled. Everything... They said it happened really fast. He was out doing his job, helping people. Serving his country. And an instant later, there was an explosion and some hate-filled psychotic murderer took my son away from me. Just like that, my baby boy was gone. I...I like to think that, as he laid there on that dirt road in the middle of that God-forsaken country... that maybe, he had one last chance to look up into the faces of the people he was trying to protect... And that he had just enough strength left to smile. And maybe Eddie's smile touched their hearts the way it always did mine. And maybe, just maybe, it made a difference...

101.

Show me the way... All I'm asking is that you help me get through this. Because I can't do it alone. I tried, but I'm all out of ideas here. It's too much. Way too much. More than I can handle. And I just feel so lost. And scared. Really scared. So please... Show me the way. Let me know what I'm supposed to do. That's all I ask...

102.

Listen, it's not you. It's not luck. It's not even all about
you. There are three or four times in everybody's life
where things completely fall apart. Everything they
believe starts to crumble before their eyes. Sudden
tragedy, a betrayal, job loss, an illness, or even a break-up
they never saw coming. It happens to all of us. We cry,
we scream, we pray, and eventually, we pull through. We
survive, because that is what we do. All we can do. Shove
our way past the awfulness and the unfairness of it all.
Then, little by little, life becomes tolerable again.
Now you and I have been through tough times before.
We suffered, but we survived. And you're going to make
it through this too. Just remember there are a lot of us
who care about you. And that sometimes, even if we
can't see it, the next chapter of our lives may not be as
dark as we think. You got this, brother. You got this.

103.

I remember the last supper I had with my family before I
left home. It wasn't anything special really. Meat loaf I
think. The same meal my mom had cooked a thousand
times. But I knew...we all knew...it would be the last time
we would all be gathered around the table together.
My childhood and adolescence were gone. My future –
ominous, ill-defined and exciting - lay before me.
And all I could do was spend one last meal with my
family before I rushed off into that wide-open void I had
chosen...

104.

You ask me why I don't trust people. I'll tell you why...
Experience. Really painful personal experience. I wasn't
always this cynical. Like everyone else, I started out wide-
eyed and gullible. Believing that deep down inside, every
person was basically good. Just a little misunderstood.
Give them a chance, show them a little respect, and
maybe even offer a helping hand and a smile...and
anybody will do the right thing. Treat you fairly. After all,
we're all part of the same species, right? The first time I
was mugged, I told the guy that I forgave him. I said he
probably needed the money more than me. When I came
to in the hospital three days later, I had a swollen face,
three cracked ribs and seventeen stitches in my stomach.
It only took me two more robberies, a stolen car, a
couple of betrayals at work, and a wife who left me for
my best friend before it suddenly dawned on me that I
might need to rethink my theory about the basic
goodness of my fellow human beings. So, don't talk to
me about trust. That was stolen from me years ago.

105.

You know all those commercials that say, "Just Do It?"
Well, they're wrong. Especially when you're a teenager.
The easiest way to guarantee a life of poverty is to get
pregnant as a teen. And when you think about all the
sexually transmitted diseases out there... it just isn't
worth it. Just Do It? I don't think so. Some things are
worth waiting for... and I'm one of them.

106.

Feel that? That little tingle in your belly? Like you are so
excited, you might turn yourself inside out at any second?
I get that same feeling every time I'm about to go on
stage. Knowing there's a whole audience out there
waiting for me to say my first word. Hoping that I'll be
so believable and so amazing, I can pull them right up
here on stage with me. Not physically, of course – I need
them to stay in their seats or it'll ruin the play – but
emotionally. I'm going to yank them out of themselves,
shake off the dust of their own boring lives and make
them laugh, cry, fall completely, crazily in love, or feel
anything I'm feeling when I'm up there on stage. That's
the beauty of acting. You're the magician, but instead of
pulling a rabbit out of a hat, you're pulling emotions out
of a hungry audience. And they love you for it! Because
they are so damn desperate to feel alive again. So
desperate to feel anything at all. And that's your gift to
them. Making them feel more than themselves. Oops.
There it is again. The tingle in the belly. That means
we're on. Let's go make some magic!

107.

Thanks for the kind words. It's nice that you're proud of
my accomplishments. And it's sweet that you want to
show me off to your friends. But the truth is… I don't
need your approval. I do what I do because that's who I
am. If I make you happy, that's wonderful. But I'm not
doing it for you. My life is my own. And I'm fine with it.

108.

It's all right. Whatever happens, it's going to be all right.
You can survive this. I know it's a cliché, but I've had a
good life. Really. For most of my life, I've woken up in
the arms of someone who loved me. I've left a little bit
of me behind in my children. And I've done more
unbelievable things than I ever thought I'd get a chance
to do. Sure, I made mistakes. Thousands of them. But
maybe I've done enough good to balance them out. Least
I hope so. It's funny. I used to imagine this would be the
most terrifying moment of my life. But it's not even
close. Terrifying was putting each of you on the bus that
very first day of school. Waiting up late at night, while
you went off to your teenage parties, leaving me all alone
to imagine every horrible thing that could happen to my
babies. And no operation could ever be as scary as when
you realize your kids are all grown up, and just don't
need you anymore. But that's how life goes. It has its
good moments, and it then has its endings. So, whatever
happens in there, I'm okay with it. And you need to be,
too.

109.

You don't know me. You think you do, but you don't.
The truth is, you know absolutely nothing about me.
Nothing… You sit there thinking you have all the
answers, but I'm a stranger to you. A complete stranger.
And you have no idea what I'm capable of.

110.

I fight the morning, pushing through the thick gauzy fog
of slumber. Not because I want to, but because the alarm
doesn't give me any choice.

I turn it off, as the inviting arms of selfish, seductive
sleep try to pull me back to their comfortable caress.
They win; I drift, then stir again. Only slightly in the
waking world. Then I hear your soft, slow breath beside
me. Feel the fiery warmth of your thigh against mine.
Open my eyes to see you curled up, one with the
mattress. You're so impossibly cute when you sleep,
rumpled hair spilling onto the pillow, your small slender
body in some awkward dance pose. I swear, I can stare at
you like this forever.

Suddenly, a tiny pout slips over your closed eye
expression. A childlike frown, escaping from a dream
that didn't go your way. Or maybe you can sense me
staring at you. Whatever the reason, it is so endearing, I
can't help but laugh. And though you still dwell deeply in
dreams, my laughter chases away the frown. Without
waking, you roll toward the sound of my voice, throw a
gentle arm across my chest.

Yesterday, you asked me what my best day was. It is this.
It is now. It's every morning I wake up to find you lying
here beside me.

That is, and always will be, my best day ever.

111.

I'm done. Finished. I give up. I can't do this anymore. After all these years, I'm tired of chasing the dream. Believing it is finally about to happen for me…only to see it all fall apart again. It's time I admit that my dreams are simply that…Dreams. Illusions. Insubstantial as ghosts. The sad truth is that I am nothing special. And it looks like I never will be.

It's funny, when I was younger, I honestly believed I was destined to do great things. I'd lie in bed, staring up at the ceiling and imagine there was some historic purpose ahead of me. A reason for my existence. Something I was meant to do. A chance to make the world a better place for my having been here. Something I'd be remembered for long after I was gone. I don't know. Maybe everyone feels that way when they're six or seven.

But I believed it. I really did.

And then there comes a point when you have to accept that it was nothing more than a childish fantasy. When you finally realize you are nothing special. A nobody. And when you die, maybe a handful of family and close friends will cry for a month or two, but nothing will change. Not really. You'll be gone, and it won't even make the news.

Anyway, time to let it go. Put it all away and admit I have wasted the vast majority of my life.

I guess that's what they mean by growing up...

112.

Love. How can you describe it? What makes it last? Sure, there's that loss of newness as the years settle in. Even the hottest fire eventually burns down to glowing embers. But there's something more. A soft conspiracy of memories shared only by the two of you. A teamwork of anger, because no matter how frustrated you may be with each other, when someone attacks you, that other person feels wounded on your behalf. And then there's the unstated blinders of familiarity. Pretending not to notice how badly you sing, or all those lazy moments you spend on the sofa. And touch. That tender arm reaching out in the still of the night. Holding you without thought or expectation. A comforting caress that tells you; there is still one place in this world where you belong. There is, and always will be, a special warmth that is yours, and yours alone. Go chase the flash and Valentines, if you want. I'll take those moments alone with someone who sees me as I really am. And loves me in spite of it.

113.

It's stalking me. This feeling that something great is gonna happen for me. It's stalking me, waiting for just the right moment to pounce and change my life forever. Maybe tomorrow. Maybe five years from now. Maybe before I finish this sentence...
Okay, maybe five years from now. But it's gonna happen. I can feel it. It's stalking me...

114.

Stay away from me. I'm poison. I don't mean to be, but I am. No matter how much I try, I ruin those I care for. Destroy the people foolish enough to fall in love with me... I don't know why, but I have never been able to find peace, or even simple contentment. Never satisfied with the many blessings I've been giving. I recognize them. Appreciate them. And even bear the burden of them. But it's not enough. It's never enough. I only pretend to be happy, while my soul quietly burns for each missed opportunity, every potential love affair... any hope of ending the boredom and irrelevancy of my life. So here I am...left to live the solid, respectable life, even as I let myself get swept away with each unexpected smile...every soft, inviting glance...and an endless series of crushes that I hide deep down inside. Even if they remain only dreams, they are still destructive. As I retreat more and more into my desperate imagination, I end up hurting those who cling to me with real hopes and fragile hearts. So, stay away from me. I'm poison. And I will only leave you even more unhappy than I am myself.

115.

I should be disappointed...but I'm not. I always knew you'd let me down eventually. That you couldn't be trusted. That's why I had you watched. Followed. You didn't know that, did you? Everywhere you went. Everyone you talked to. Everything you did… I know it all. So, don't even try to deny it. Don't even try.

116.

I don't know much. No one would ever mistake me for a philosopher. I don't have the time, the temperament, or the talent for big thoughts. But there is one thing I learned, and I learned it the hard way...
No one cares. The universe is deaf to your questions and complaints. There ain't no 'Great Plan' that I can see. Crying and pleading amount to just shy of nothing in this world. So why waste your breath?
You go sharpen your knife. Face up to the circumstances you're thrown into. Or you die.
Simple as that.

117.

First time in the joint, huh? I can tell. First-timers always got that "I don't deserve to be in here" look in their eye. Like any of us do. Well, maybe some do. Those cats down in cellblock six, they don't deserve to be any place real people are. Those cats, they'd grab ya fast, chew you up and crap you out without thinkin' twice 'bout it. So, you stay far away from them, y'hear?
So whatta ya in for, kid? Me, I'm doin' a nickel plus for B&E. I didn't do it, of course. I'm innocent, like most of us model citizens in here. Victims of a justice system that can't tell a con from a cornhole.
Except those cretins in cell block six. Those dudes ain't even on the same mental planet as the rest of us. You remember what I told you and stay clear of 'em, y'hear?

118.

I'm addicted to you. Lord knows, I don't want to be. I hate waiting for the phone to ring, or the sound of the doorknob turning. I can't stand being so dependent on seeing your smile. Sharing the day's news. Or simply hearing your voice. But the truth is, there is life…and there is life with you in it. And whether I get to see you for one minute, or talk to you for an hour, nobody can flood happiness into my day like you can. And I guess if I have to be addicted to anything, I'm glad it's you.

119.

You think it's easy being me? The athlete. The jock. The superstar on the field or the court? Let me tell you…it's not. If you're good at sports, people always assume your dumb. They don't mean to, but sometimes even teachers act surprised when I ace a test. I think Miss Frankel is convinced I'm cheating somehow. But I'm not. I study hard. I have to, because it doesn't come easy to me. Not like the brainy kids. And my Dad pushes and pushes me so hard to be the best. Always yelling at me to toughen up… There's so much pressure playing sports. I have to train and work out and show up for practice and eat a certain way. Some days, all I want to do is sit back and chill. But I can't. Because being me means I'm only as good as my last touchdown. I'm only liked when I win the game. Other people mess up, they don't put it in the newspaper. Me? I'm just one fumble away from being the big loser they talk about for the rest of the season.

120.

How can you talk to her like that? She doesn't deserve your disrespect, especially after all she's done for you. All the heartache and misery you dump on her. All that crap she takes from you without a single complaint. And why? Because you need to feel better by tearing somebody else down? Or because you feel so unlovable, you have to torture anyone who has the nerve to love you in spite of yourself? Honestly, I don't care why you feel you have to treat her like that. But if I ever hear you talking to her, or anyone else like that again, you'll have to deal with me. And then I'll show you what real suffering is....

121.

So, here's how it's gonna go. I'm gonna cut you right here. Just a small slice. Not deep enough to sever any major vein or artery, so I don't have to worry about you bleeding out just yet. But it'll hurt. Believe me, it'll hurt. Then I'll wait twenty seconds or so. Enough time for you to fully experience all that delicious anguish. Then I'll make the next cut here. Small, surgical, precise, but exquisitely painful. And every twenty seconds I'll make another and another and another, until your mind screams in agony.

The Chinese call it death by a thousand cuts. But I think I can get a coupla thousand slices in before you give up the ghost...

So, what do you say? Shall we get started?

122.

You let me down. I know you didn't mean to, and maybe I expected too much from you. But you let me down. You let me down and it hurt. Ever since I was little, I looked up to you. To me, you were everything.

Oh, I know what everyone was saying. I heard the rumors. I even saw you doing things you swore you'd never do. And each time, I'd make excuses for you. She's been through a lot. She's under a lot of pressure. The pills are only for the pain. She doesn't take them every day. Besides, people don't understand what she's going through. If only I could make it easier for her.

But I can't make it easier for you. And I can't lie for you anymore. You're an addict. You're an addict and you use people. Me, most of all.

So, keep your stories to yourself. I'm done with you.

123.

I don't know what happened tonight. I don't understand the how or why. Maybe we never will. For all I know, it could have been a miracle, a coincidence, or just a dream we all lived through... But there is one thing I do know... The almighty Creator of the universe doesn't need our belief to make him any more or less real. He doesn't need any tricks or objects to intervene on our behalf. He hears our cries in the night. He knows our guilt and our pain. And He desperately wants us to heal. He so desperately wants us to heal....

124.

The way I see it, there are times you make it on brains and talent. And times you make it by sleeping your way up the ladder. Me? I'm gonna climb to the top on sheer guts and ruthlessness. I have absolutely no problem being a stone-cold winner, who doesn't give a damn about how many bodies I have to step over on to get there. So, you can either help me make it to the top…or prepare to get crushed under my heel as I leave you behind. Your call, man. Your call.

125.

You doing okay? Those cuffs not too tight? Well, that's too bad. Y'see, the boys in this precinct don't have much sympathy for scumbags like you that rob old people of their social security checks. So, here's how it's gonna go down. You're gonna sit here until you realize what a piss-awful situation you're in, and decide to do the smart thing, giving up your scumbag partners before they make a deal and give you up. Or you can ask for a lawyer and get some court-appointed hack just out of law school, who'll look at your file for a whole two minutes, before running home to bang his wife and watch Law & Order reruns on TV. He's not gonna get you any better deal than this one…spill your guts and take two years or stay stupid and go away for a long time. Your choice...

126.

I used to have this dream. Every night, the same one. I'm walking down this endless, dark hall, barefoot, on a floor that's cold and shiny as a razor blade. I'm looking for you, but I can't find you anywhere. I can't find anyone. I'm all alone, except suddenly, there's something or someone, crushing my chest with these cold, icy claws. The shadows are closing in on me, and I can't see who or what is trying to squeeze the air out of my lungs... I gasp, and gurgle and struggle to breathe, and I just know there's no way I 'm making it out of this hall alive. No way at all. I don't know why, but I'm afraid to look behind me. I know something's there. Something bad. But I can't turn my head. My neck doesn't work anymore. My neck is gone. Doesn't exist anymore. I stretch my eyes down to see that I'm buried up to my chin in the floor, and that...whatever it is behind me, is getting closer.
Closer... Ever closer...
I can't breathe because it'll hear me, 'cause the choking sound in my own throat is so unbelievable loud it hurts my ears. Just then, the walls drop away, and everything is pitch black darkness, crawling with these evil little things I can't see, but I can hear. I hear them scuttering and slithering towards me...
Closer... Ever closer...
as I'm buried neck deep in the floor, and can't move to save myself...
Pretty scary, huh?

127.

There is a point you reach in life. A moment when you
suddenly realize the world is hostile… foreign… and
cold. All those safe illusions of childhood are shattered.
Your parents aren't all powerful. There's nobody
watching out for you. And the things you do without
thinking can have consequences that will haunt you every
day for the rest of your life.

It started out as just another night, partying with my
friends. I knew these streets like the back of my hand.
Every side street, every crack of pavement had some
familiar childhood memory etched into it. I belonged
here. This neighborhood was my skin, the outer layer of
my soul. This was my world and I was safe here.

At least until she stepped off the curb…

It was dark, and she came outta nowhere. She didn't even
look before she walked into the street. Even if I hadn't
been drinking, it still would've been impossible to stop in
time. Kids her age should know better. They should
know better…

Nobody looks at me the same anymore. I don't look at
myself the same way. I'm not the familiar face, the party
person that used to make everyone laugh. Now I'm the
tragic mistake. The reckless driver. The stealer of life…

Like I said, there's a point you reach in life. A moment
when you suddenly realize the world is hostile…
foreign… and cold. And the things you do without
thinking can haunt you for the rest of your life.

128.

It's funny. You think you know a person. You think you share the same values, the same goals... But the truth is, you really never do. People are people. And that's not always a good thing... But then someone like you comes along, and...well, it starts to make me trust people again. And it makes me happy. You...make me happy.

129.

There was a point yesterday, when you weren't even looking at me. We were at that office party, and you were so caught up in everything going on around us. Listening to the people on your left rambling on about the latest financial crisis or celebrity split-up, or whatever they were babbling about. And you looked right past me, as if I was invisible. Completely invisible. But then, you slipped your hand under the table and touched my knee. It wasn't anything sexual, or maybe it was. It was just so sweet and soft, and spontaneous and...and real. As if this casual little touch said you belonged to me, and I belonged to you, and all that chatter going on meant nothing. Just that one little touch, for not even five seconds, made me feel like I mattered in this world. Like I mattered to you. After that, I didn't care what anybody else said. Someone felt comfortable enough to reach out, to let me know through the silent poetry of your fingertips, that you needed me near enough to touch. And that I was anything but invisible to you.

130.

Don't say it. Please, just spare me the indignity of having to listen to that ridiculous story and those same excuses again. Don't make me feel guilty for doubting what we both know are complete lies and total fabrications. You know I only pretend to believe you. And I know that you only pretend to care whether I do or not... You have a problem, Chris. Maybe you can't help yourself. But even worse than your problem is my pathetic, all-consuming, soul-crushing addiction to you. I let myself get stepped on, lied to and robbed of all dignity...in exchange for those few moments when you wrap your arms around me in the dark, and we both try to forget what a deeply destructive force you are in my life. Love isn't blind. It's cold and it's cruel, but it always knows exactly what it's doing. Like I know exactly what I'm doing by letting you back into my life. And I'm willing to let you use me and walk all over me again and again...as long as I can keep some little undamaged part of you in my life. Only please don't tell me another one of your stories. That's all I ask.

131.

Where did the time go? One moment, you're anxious and fidgety because it's taking too long to get your license, graduate from school, turn twenty-one...and set off on your own. Then everything picks up speed and blurs on by. And now, I look back over more decades gone than years to come. Wondering...Where did the time go?

132.

I hate what you do to me. How you make me feel this
way. How easy it is for you to just jerk me back and forth
with every soft smile, or simple look of disapproval. And
the worst part is, you don't even know it. You have no
clue how much control you have over my life. How
much I depend on you to give me meaning. To give me
definition…or hope. The truth is, I'm not even sure you
know my name. But I have loved you forever. Every
second of every day, of every month of every year. And
someday, one of these days, I'm just going to walk right
up to you and introduce myself. And in that very
moment when our eyes meet for the first time, you'll find
out how much you love me. Right then and there, you'll
fall head over heels in love with me. I know you will.
You'll have to. You'll just have to…

133.

I have to tell you something. I couldn't sleep at all last
night. Not a bit. I just laid there, all alone in those soft,
silky sheets, and thought of you. How beautiful your eyes
are. How warm and caring every time they look at me.
And that sweet smile of yours that makes me weak in the
knees. I thought of your lips, and imagined how soft
they would be to kiss. One long, lingering kiss that starts
out friendly, almost by accident, but then gets so deep
and steamy, it takes our breath away. Anyway, that's why
I couldn't sleep last night. And it's all your fault…

134.

It's a hard thing. A hard, hard thing. Lyin' awake all
night, feelin' way too small in this oversized bed. Just you
trapped inside those four suffocating walls, in a life too
small by half. Knowin' deep in your bones, that you're all
alone in this world. That all the things you thought you
was doin' right somehow led up to this. Bein' by yourself.
Shut out from the rest of the world. And no one to give
a second thought as to whether you're still drawin' breath
the whole night long, or whether you'll up and die,
unmourned in your bed before first mornin' light.
Alone, you know, really alone, don't necessarily mean
nobody's around. Really alone is like there's somebody,
anybody, who should be there with you in that room…in
that bed, but ain't. Instead, there's this cold, empty space
where a shadow of a real person used to be, but ain't no
more. Like they been up and erased. That long piece of
no one has a human shape around its coal black
emptiness. You can almost see it. Almost feel it, 'cause it
creates this icy vacuum that drives straight into your
chest, turnin' your heart inside out. Even more so, 'cause
you know you did this to yourself. You're to blame. You
put that vacuum in your heart. You made that bed
empty. You erased that somebody from your life. All
those somebodies, that should have been there beside
you, but ain't. It's a hard thing. But there you are. You
gotta live with it. Or not. And either way, it won't matter
to a damn soul. Not a damn soul in this world.

135.

Hey. Trust me. This stuff is non-addictive, non-invasive, non-habit forming and nothing but pure pleasure. You try it and BAM…it's like you're instantly invincible, untouchable and ready to live forever. We're talking sweetness and light straight to your bloodstream. So, forget what Mommy and Daddy say. Time to roll up your sleeve and plug into the universe. Fifty bucks a hit. Danger free and exultation guaranteed. Nothing bad can happen. Trust me. You know you can trust me…

136.

Do you ever wonder what it's going to be like after you're gone? I mean, they'll all be sad for the first year or two. A few people who really loved you will cry whenever your name is mentioned. Then the tears will turn into soft, distant memories. Somebody'll tell a story about some dopey thing you did, and everyone will smile with affection. But then they'll move on. Life always moves on. In a few more years, they'll only think of you on Memorial Day and maybe a Christmas or two. And then the people who remember you will start to die off themselves. In fifty years, you'll be nothing more than a half-remembered name on a family tree…a fading scratch on a tombstone. After that, it'll be like you were never here at all. Nothing you did, nothing you said, nothing you thought…will have mattered at all. Dust to dust. Memory to irrelevance. That's what we all have to look forward to.

137.

It's wrong, isn't it? My feeling like this? I know it's
wrong. I try to avoid you. Try to keep away. Try to stop
thinking of you. But I can't help it. When something
good happens, you're the first person I want to share it
with. When everything falls apart, you're the first person
I run to. The only place I feel safe. I know it's wrong, but
I can't help it. You're an addiction for me. An irresistible
hunger. And I can't get enough of you. I just can't...

138.

People think you have to be by yourself to feel alone. But
they're wrong. The worst kind of alone is when you're
surrounded by other people... even those you love... and
you can't seem to make them understand how lonely you
feel inside. Like there's this great glass wall of pain and
regret that locks you away from the world. You can see
them, they can see you... but we're shadows to each
other. Too distant to feel or touch. Somewhere, years
ago, I just lost my way. The more I distracted myself with
what I wanted to be, what I wanted to do... the more I
seemed to slip away from what I really was. Until I
became as much a shadow to myself as everyone else
seemed to me. Now, each day pulls me further out to
sea. Each empty moment drags me deeper under water. I
can see sunlight glinting off the waves above me, but my
arms are too tired to fight my way back to the
surface...And I wish to God there was somebody or
something there to help pull me back to shore...

139.

There is evil in the world. I know it. You may think
everyone is basically good, but there are more people out
there willing to stab you in the back than you think. Who
would happily crush your dreams and destroy your life,
then lie right to your face about how sorry they are for
your troubles. But don't believe them. They want you to
fail. To go down in flames. That's what makes them
happy. And the worst part about evil is, you never see it
coming. It's the ones you trust. The one's you would do
anything for. Those are the ones that will kill you. Kill
you in a heartbeat.
Believe me, I know. It happened to me, more times than
I can count...
Which is why I don't feel that bad about getting you
fired. I know you didn't steal that money, but someone
had to take the blame, and it was either you or me. And
no way I was going down for it. So, I planted half the
money in your desk, and told the boss it was you.
Kinda evil, I guess, but like I said...there is evil in the
world, you know?

140.

Enough. I don't give a damn what you say. I don't care
what you think. I don't care about you at all. You crossed
a line this time, and there's no going back from this. Just
get out of here. I never want to see you again. Ever. So,
get out of my life. I hate you. I really hate you.

141.

Do you ever see ants? I mean, really look at them? Ants in the same colony all look alike. Maybe not to each other, but to me. They all move in a single file like little robot clones. Following the ant in front of them, even if they have no idea where any of them are going. School is a lot like that. Everybody tries so hard to look the same. And there's all this pressure to follow the popular kids, even if they're idiots and do stupid things. I saw this video once. Some researchers plucked a couple of ants from their nest, and gave them a different scent, or some chemical to make them act different from the rest. Then they put them back in with the others. Only the normal ants didn't like the different ones. They ignored them and marched away, single file. Leaving them behind. Or sometimes, they attacked them. Just because they were different. Maybe it was different in the old days. But school isn't a place of learning anymore. It's an ant farm. And the only ones smart enough to realize it end up getting ignored or attacked. Believe me, I know.

142.

Don't pretend like you know me. You don't. Nobody does. Sometimes, I don't even know myself. That may sound funny to you, but it's not funny to me. Not funny at all. From where I'm sitting, this is all one big pain in the you-know-what, and it don't look like it's ever going to get any better. Y'know what I mean?

143.

I can't wait for Thursday. I can't wait to see that look on
her face. You don't know how long I've been planning
this. And finally, it all comes together this Thursday
night. Six PM. Ready or not.

See, Marissa and I used to be close. Best friends. I could
tell her anything and I usually did. What I didn't know
was that she was passing it along to everybody else in
town. And not the way I told her. No, she liked to
embellish things. Change the facts around to make a
better story. And to make me look worse. While I was
sharing my innermost feelings with her, she was twisting
them into dirty little secrets and using them as
entertainment for her much more popular friends.

It took me a long time to understand all the giggles and
whispers. Total strangers laughing behind my back barely
loud enough for me to hear. Marissa denied it, of course.
But eventually, some of my friends... my real friends...
told me what she was doing. It hurt for a long time. I
thought I'd never get over the hurt. The shame. The
betrayal. But hey, times change. People grow up. We get
over it. And now we have the internet. And those little
bitty cameras. So, in four days, when Marissa sneaks
around for her regular Thursday night affair with
Tiffany's husband. I won't say a word. I'll just email the
images to everyone she knows.

So, if you're not doing anything this Thursday night at
six, log onto *www.revenge-is-sweet.com.*

144.

There's nothing left for us anymore. Everything we planned on, everything we believed in, all our hopes and dreams… All gone. When the bank shut us down, they did more than kill a business. They killed the best part of you and me. Twenty years of hard work gone. Just like that. Twenty years of blood and sweat thrown away, because of one stupid lawsuit that would have been dismissed if the judge wasn't sleeping with the plaintiff's cousin. But am I bitter? No. Sometimes the universe just needs a victim, and it was our turn, I guess. That's all. Our turn to have our dreams crushed. Just our turn...

145.

Let me tell you something. There is Authority, and there is Power. Authority is that naggy, whiny voice you hear when some self-important little man has a whole passel of rules behind him. He thinks you have to listen to him, because he can make life damn uncomfortable for you. And he has others telling him what rules to follow, or they'll make his life damn uncomfortable too.
But Power…Power don't need to nag. It don't need rules, or people who believe they're way more important than they are. Power is a force all by itself. Now when I break your arm, it's not because I want to make you uncomfortable. It's to make you think twice about repossessing my car. You have the Authority. I have a baseball bat. Let's see which one has more Power, okay?

146.

There's a reason they call it space. It's so unbelievably…
empty. I know that's a cliché, but you can't really grasp it
until you're up here. Alone. With nothing left to hold
onto. Not even hope. The bright, burning sun…warm to
everybody but me. Its searing light impotent against the
icy blackness squeezing my chest. Gasp by gasp. A billion
stars, distant as the fading memory of my wife's embrace.
And that painfully perfect, blue swirl of Earth hanging in
the darkness. Mocking me… Enormous. Unreachable…
Tempting with the sweet promise of safety. Of home.
Over seven billion people, stupidly oblivious under their
smothering ocean of air. While I watch the uncaring
gauges on my own dwindling atmosphere tick off my few
remaining breaths.
I'm sweating inside this artificial skin, drifting slowly
away from Earth. Away from the torn carcass of my ship.
Away from everything I ever loved, ever wanted, and was
too distracted to appreciate while I had them within
arm's reach.
And when that last stale air in my suit finally thins out
enough to burn my lungs… three-point-two-five hours
from now…I'll drift further and further away.
One more lifeless object in space.
Surrounded by darkness…
Touching nothing…
…forever…

147.

Why do I do it? Can't really say. Some people play music or sports. Some cook, play cards, go to movies, or hang out with their friends. I kill people. It's just what I do. At the trial, my lawyer came up with this whole litany of familiar excuses… Tragic childhood. Isolation. It was society's fault, not mine. But that's just what the jury wanted to hear. You see, normal people need a way to understand someone like me. It makes them feel better. Makes them feel they are different from the cold-blooded monster with the everyday face. Hey, whatever gets them through the night. As for me, I'm not even sure I enjoy it anymore. The killing. It's more of a compulsion. So, I guess it is better I'm locked up in here. All this concrete and steel separating me from the rest of the world. Because I'm pretty sure if they do ever let me go…if I was ever free to roam your streets… I'd do it again, and again and again. It's what I do.

148.

Don't cry for me. I raised you better'n that. I brought you up to stand strong and face any challenge that comes. And that's all this is. Just one more challenge I gotta face. You wipe all those tears away right now. They ain't doin' anyone any good. And you stand up strong, like I taught you. You throw those shoulders back, grit your teeth and you remember your old man never shrank back from nothin'. So, don't you cry for me. No matter what happens. Don't you cry. Just don't…

149.

Will it ever be enough? The things I do? The awards?
The accomplishments? The approval I've been so
desperately seeking ever since I was a kid? It all looks
great on paper. Gets me the embarrassing compliments,
or the occasional flirtation that fools my heart into
thinking maybe I can feel something...feel anything
again. Maybe I matter. But when I stumble back into my
apartment - head-throbbing and exhausted - and climb
into that big, empty bed...all those compliments ring
hollow. The accomplishments don't mean anything. And
another long, lonely night mocks every dream, every
hope and everything I ever thought I'd be. Big man?
Naw. Just another broken soul all alone. Nothing more.

150.

Why do you talk to me like that? Making me feel like
everything I do is wrong, and everything I say is stupid?
When did it change from you wanting me to be around,
to you not being able to sit in the same room without
finding a dozen or more things you can't stand about
me? I can't even remember the last time I saw you smile,
you gave me a compliment, or even asked how my day
was and then actually listened to what I said.
Okay, maybe everything I do is wrong. Maybe everything
I say is stupid. That doesn't mean you have to tell me
that, twenty-four-seven.
Or am I wrong about that too?

151.

I can't move. I want to, but I can't. My feet are heavy.
Like they're glued to the floor. It's been nine minutes
since I lost control over half my body. I know that
because I'm frozen here, staring up at the kitchen clock.
Nine horrible, horrifying minutes, and it's spreading.
Spreading like death, with only the back of this chair
keeping me from falling over. My right arm hangs
uselessly to the ground, and the left is tingling and
turning numb. I can't feel my legs anymore. I try to
scream, but don't have the strength to pry open my lips.
And even if I could, there's not nearly enough breath in
me to make a sound. Feels like there's nothing left in me
at all. I'm fading. Bit by bit. I'm fading away. And I don't
even know why. Lord, help me, I don't even know why...

152.

Okay, there's me, and there is this person everyone
expects me to be. Sometimes it's easier to be that other
person. Always polite. Always happy. Always liking the
same things everyone tells me I should like.
But other times, it feels like the real me is trapped inside
this suffocating hard shell, screaming to get out. Because
I'm not always happy. I'm not into sports, or clothes, or
who's dating who, or even how I'm supposed to act to
be accepted.
Maybe being accepted isn't that big a deal. Maybe
accepting the real me inside is more important than what
everybody else thinks. But what do I know?

153.

Dear Diary…

…it's Monday again, and that means I have exactly four days left to hear all my friends talk about how much fun they're going to have this weekend.

Jessica's going to the game with Dave. Drew and Jacob are going over his house to play Xbox…at least that's what Drew's gonna tell her parents. Mandy and Claire are double-dating to some slasher movie festival with Steve and Keith.

And me, I'll sit at home yet again. Babysitting my little sister and listening to my Mom asking me over and over why I don't have friends like everybody else.

The thing is, I don't know why I don't have friends like everyone else. I don't know why I never get asked out, or invited to all the cool parties, or even have people notice I'm alive at all.

I've got a little sister who's spoiled, a Facebook page with only six friends, and a cell phone that never rings. And a stupid Diary that's the only one who knows how sad and lonely I really am.

Dear Diary, I'm sorry I called you stupid. You're the best friend I have. You're probably the only real friend I have. I'll write more tomorrow.

But don't expect it to be any more exciting than this.

154.

There's no such thing as monsters. That's what everyone tells you. Just stories they tell us as kids to scare us into being good. Not stay up too late at night or go too far from home. Parenting by terror, I guess. And you know Hollywood is always there to cash in whatever way they can. Vampires. Zombies. Slimy, ugly creatures straight out of nightmares that can never be killed. They keep coming. That's what makes them monsters. No matter what you do, they just keep coming. As for me, I'm not afraid of vampires or zombies. It's real evil that scares me. The kind of evil that turns ordinary people into killers. Makes them blame each other for all the unfair things in their lives. Teaches them to hate. To cut off heads in the Middle East. Kidnap young girls in Africa. Turn little children into suicide bombers. Bombing and butchering, and believing they have every right to do so. Like murdering innocent people is some kind of righteous act. Those are the real monsters. And God help us, there are more and more of them every day.

155.

Listen. We do this, and we're square with the boss. He forgets all about the screw-up in the alley, and we don't catch a bullet for dumping his stash. All we have to do is carry this bag down to an address downtown. We can't look in it. That's gospel. We deliver it by midnight, and maybe we can stop running. This is our last chance to make it right with him. We screw this up, and we're dead.

156.

I'm not me anymore. At least not the me I always
thought I was. The person everyone told me I should be.
It took me all this time to realize I had become this
strange collection of behaviors that had nothing to do
with who I was deep inside. I was simply a reflection of
everyone else's wants and beliefs. The rules my parents
lived by. The prejudices of my hometown. The politics
of my education. The family and friends I tried to please.
Even the books that told me how I should live my life.
Let everyone I met define me. Every time someone said,
"That's not like you," I made sure it wasn't. With all that
pressure, I lost me. I forgot who I really was. And now, I
have no idea who that person is...

157.

It's funny. I thought it would be worse than this. More
quiet. More alone. But it really isn't that bad. It's like Rick
is still here with me. Sometimes when I walk into a room,
I can almost feel him next to me. Telling me everything is
going to be all right. Like last night, when I rolled over
onto his side of the bed, I could have sworn I felt him
kiss my cheek. I mean, I know he's been gone all these
years, but maybe...just maybe we leave a little piece of
ourselves behind in the places we love the most. With the
people we love the most. Like one last hug that never
quite fades away. Anyway, that's what it feels like to me.
And knowing that makes it easier to get through each day
without him. Is that so bad?

158.

How could he do this? We were his friends. We hung out together ever since third grade. He slept over my house, and we used to terrorize my big sister by putting dead ants, cinnamon and ground up crayons in her makeup. All summer long, we played video games until three in the morning. Did everything together... Until he started to get angry at everyone. I don't know why. He kept getting in fights, and even yelling at teachers. I tried to ask him what was up, but all he kept saying was how he hated his classes and everyone in them. And today that idiot brought his dad's gun to school. I'm glad the janitor grabbed it before he did something even more stupid. But who knows what he would have done if Mr. Weston wasn't there? Kill some kids? Kill me? People change, but you never expect your best friends could turn into something like that. I mean, how could he do this?

159.

You think you know me? What makes me tick? What I'm feeling inside? You don't know a thing about me. You have no idea what I'm feeling. And the truth is, you don't really care. I could get hit by a car, and you'd cry for exactly two-minutes-twenty. Say a few words of pity. Smile at something I said years ago, or some dope thing you remember I did. And then it's old news. You'd never give me another thought. So, tell me...since you think you know me...why do I take it? Why do I keep coming back to you? Because I sure as hell can't figure it out...

160.

Look, I know you're scared. The truth is, I'm a little scared myself. But this could be anything. Anything at all. And it could even be nothing. So, it doesn't make any sense for us to get all upset and teary-eyed until we know exactly what's happening. Until we know what we're up against here. Like I said, it could be nothing at all, but... just in case it isn't... I want you to know that I can handle it. I can handle anything that comes along. As long as I have you beside me. So, dry those eyes of yours. Go get dressed in something really special. I'm taking you out to that ridiculously expensive Italian restaurant you love so much. We are going to drink champagne we can't afford, and flirt in public like it's our very first date. We are not even going to think about this thing. Not once. Instead, we are going to count our blessings while we have them. Because my biggest blessing is you. Nothing else matters. Okay?

161.

Isn't that just like life these days? You start to get to know someone... Begin to peer through the carefully constructed fog of social construct and peer pressure personality to finally grab a glimpse of who they really are...and suddenly, they move on, as someone new shows up to distract you and begin the process all over again. Nobody stays where or who they are for long. We move...no, run...to catch up with some impossible vision of our lives. And I'm just so tired of running...

162.

I know they're out there. Hiding. Watching. Waiting.
They sit just past the edge of darkness, past the point you
can see them. Where you can barely hear them. But I
know they're out there. Bleeding out of the shadows like
they have no substance, no form. Disappearing into the
night the second your eye catches sight of them. They do
that so you doubt yourself. That's what they want. That's
what they feed on. Doubt. Doubt and complacency. But
not me. I know they're out there. Creeping and scuttling
around on so many twisted, inhuman legs. Waiting for
until my back is turned. Waiting for my guard to drop.
Waiting for the moment I close my eyes to sleep. And in
that terrifying split-second, they'll be all over me. Wave
after wave. Swarming over my legs, my chest, my face.
Tearing my flesh. Feeding on my warm. Sucking the life
out of me. Until I…'til I… I… So, don't you dare tell me
they're not they're out there. Don't tell me they're not
real. I know what I know. And I know they're waiting for
me. Just past the edge of darkness...

163.

Nobody talks to each other anymore. We've got our
iPods, iPads, iPhones, headphones, ear buds, and a
hundred other ways to shut people out with the latest
noise and gossip. We hide behind electronic walls of
unsocial social media, then turn to some online poll to
teach us how to improve our relationships. Case in
point…Do you even know my name? Well, do you?

164.

I know what the meaning of life is. I know it sounds funny, but I really do. All my life, my eyes were glued to the things I had, the things I worked for. Great career, huge house, fast car, bulging 401k, the best clothes, even a $300 haircut. That was my life. The sum of the things I bought. Nothing more. I was a man on paper. A walking balance sheet. A list of assets that just happened to live and breathe on occasion. And then I met Linda. Linda with her sarcastic smile and wide-open eyes that looked right through everything I had and saw straight to the emptiness in my chest. Of course, I flashed all the prestige and high-powered toys, and that just made her crinkle her nose and laugh, as if I were talking baby talk, while she was trying to explain philosophy to me. But she didn't really explain anything. Not with words. Linda had a way of uplifting everyone she met. With a smile. A look of encouragement. Sometimes just a comfortable silence that let them know she understood and that she was there. Linda couldn't be bought, and that frustrated the hell out of me. Frustrated me for months. Until finally, I asked her what the hell she wanted from me? She just laughed and said "Nothing you can buy on credit…" Our marriage only lasted seven months. The cancer took her much quicker than the doctors had said it would. But every day I looked into her amazing eyes and saw the peace and the love in them…Every day I looked into her eyes…I saw the meaning of life. Felt it in my heart. And believe me, it's nothing you can buy on credit.

165.

I've been on my own six years now. Six years since I last
kissed my mother and father good-bye, then set out to
make the life I wanted. I left right after Christmas,
because I knew how much having family around for the
holidays meant to Mom and Dad... Meant to me...
I haven't been back since. I had to prove to myself that I
could make it on my own. And I did. I have a good job.
A great apartment and lots of friends. I have everything I
ever wanted in life.
But what I can't understand is why I feel... like something
is missing, you know?
Sometimes, late at night, there's this icy, shudder-like
feeling in my chest. Like an emptiness just dying to eat its
way out. Like the walls in my apartment are a little too
close... A little too frightening.
Don't get me wrong. There's nothing the matter with my
life. I don't believe in loneliness. I can handle anything
the world throws my way.
But just once, I'd like to remember that warm, safe
feeling of being wrapped up in my mother's gentle arms.
To have her softly kiss away all my tears and make me
feel like I matter... really matter... to someone in this cold
and empty world.
Like I said, there's nothing wrong with my life. But the
other day, I heard the song "I'll Be Home for Christmas"
on the radio. And I started crying for no reason.
No reason at all...

166.

I'm tired, Jesse. Tired of the pain. There's this dark wave of weariness that goes deep as the bones and just shakes me and shudders me and feels like it's squeezin' all the life straight out of me. Maybe that don't make no sense, but none of this does. I mean, I lived a good long life. I done enough things. I sinned some, sure, but I tried to lend a hand anytime I could. I'm not sayin' I been a saint, 'cuz there's plenty better'n me. But there's plenty worse'n me, too. I'm just so damn tired of havin' everything on me ache. Tired of gaspin' and gulpin' for air, when once I coulda run from here to Aunt Jillian's house without so much as breakin' a sweat. I was somethin' back then. And that only makes it tougher to end up like this. To be like I am now. I ain't scared, Jesse. Well, maybe a little. But I just don't have the strength to hurt no more. So, it's time you let me go, Jesse. It's time you let me go...

167.

Why do I feel so numb? So empty? As if all I'm doing is playing a part. Pretending to belong here. Pretending to belong anywhere? Can't any of them see through this smile I'm wearing? Anybody at all? They're all sitting at the table. Laughing, joking. Sharing all those wonderful joys and memories, and somehow believing I share them too. But I don't. I'm a stranger here. In the middle of all these people who are supposed to matter to me…I'm alone. I'm alone, and they don't even see it. I am a stranger in my own life…and nobody knows it but me.

168.

It was yesterday morning. You were standing in the kitchen. Not doing anything special. Just loading the dishwasher. Lost in your own world, as you rinsed off and put away our coffee cups. And then suddenly, you had this soft, secret smile creep across your face. I almost didn't notice it at first. Just a little upturn at the corner of your mouth… That's all. But it showed me something I hadn't seen in a long time. A peace. A contentment. Like this simple act of having a morning cup of coffee with me was…enough for you. That it was all you needed to feel right with the world. And suddenly, I had this overwhelming desire to take you in my arms and cry into your shoulder. For that smile. For that quiet happiness. And for the reminder of why I love you so very much…

169.

You've changed my life, you know that? Before I met you, there wasn't a thing in this world that mattered to me. Not really. I'd get up in the morning and go through my day like I was sleepwalking. I didn't smile. I didn't laugh. Didn't care…but you changed all that.
Now I do the most boring things…and I smile every time I think of you. I'm driving in my car, and suddenly burst out laughing over some cute thing you said last week or the night before. And just when I didn't think I could ever feel anything for anyone…you proved me wrong. Thank you for that. Thank you so much…

170.

I know what you're thinking. I can tell by the way you look at me. You're wondering what kind of monster am I? What kind of person could do what I did…what they say I did…and still sleep at night?

I…I gave up sleeping a long time ago. Because the second I closed my eyes, my head would fill with these pictures…these dark images that don't belong in anyone's head. Especially mine.

But no matter what they say, I didn't mean to do it. I'm not saying they didn't deserve it. Every single one of them. I'm not saying those last few seconds of terror weren't good for them…or that it's sometimes really beneficial for a person's character to beg and plead so hard that sweat pours out their eyes. I'm not saying that. All I'm saying is I didn't mean to do it. That's all.

171.

So where am I supposed to go now? I can't stay here. Everyone I know either hates me or is too embarrassed to be seen with me. I can't go back home. It's been years since I left. I'd be more like a stranger. A curiosity. Some sweet, tragic memory that came back to life, even though you wished it wouldn't. We like our memories safe and sterile. Locked in the distant past, where they can't make us feel uncomfortable. We prefer those we can leave behind, and pull out only when we want to feel all misty and nostalgic. But nobody's going to feel misty about me. So, tell me… Where do I go now?

172.

Okay, I know I sound like one of those old people that I always used to roll my eyes over. But tell me, where does the time go? One moment, I'm looking out over endless years to come, anxious and fidgety because it's taking way too long until I can drive a car, graduate from school, and set off on my own. Then there are those few great and terrifying years where I finally have the chance to find out what I wanted to do in life, and who I wanted to share it with. That's when life should hit the pause button. Instead, it picks up speed, and everything around you blurs by, like mailboxes racing past car windows. All you can do is hold on tight, to keep from falling over in the dizzying rush of missed opportunities. Now, here I am, looking back on more decades wasted than years to come. Confronting all the dreams I'll never realize. All the things I meant to do, but never did. Where does the time go? And why the hell did it have to fly by so fast?

173.

It wasn't always like this, you know. People used to be proud of their neighborhoods. Real communities, where you were connected to everyone else on the block. You knew their business and they knew yours. Your family and their family were connected by decades of cookouts, gossip and adjoining back yards. Now, all we have are subdivisions, where you live next to people for years without ever knowing their names, or even the ages of their kids. We just didn't know how good we had it.

174.

I know you're out there. I can hear you smile. I can feel your presence in the dark. Waiting for me, while I lie here, waiting for you. I know the sweet smell of your hair. The twinkling sound of your laughter. Know exactly what sets your eyes on fire, and everything that makes you melt into my arms. I know your gestures, your expressions, the curve of your neck and every line of your face. I know them, even though I've never met you outside of my dreams. Outside of my heart. But I know you exist, because life would be unbearable if you aren't real. If you aren't here to share it with me. So, all I ask is that you be real. And that one day, you will come find me. Wherever you are, my love…come find me.

175.

I was trying to think of the perfect moment of my day. When I feel warm and safe and appreciated. It's not when people say nice things about me…although you know I'll always grab a compliment when I can. It's not when I stand on stage and hear applause rolling towards me, knowing that something I've done has brought a few hundred strangers to their feet. It's not the feet up on the desk, the boat slithering through the waves, or the home-cooked meal worthy of a five-star restaurant. No. The perfect moment for me is at night. Curled up in bed, with your arm thrown over me, and your soft, whispery breaths of sleep settling in my ear. That's when I feel safe. That's when I know I belong…

176.

Everyone suffers to some degree. That's the cruel, unspoken secret of life. For even those who consider themselves blessed choose not to acknowledge the million small curses that await them. Yet the joyous engine of humanity lies in our wondrous ability to endure these periodic ravages with courage, humor, or hopeful defiance. Turning tragedy into incremental victory with the sublime stubbornness of our species. A logic-defying belief that we can, and will, survive any and all challenges that befall us. And somehow - armed only with this foolish declaration of bravado - more often than not...we do. The flood waters slowly recede. The illness gradually loses its power over us. The much-feared loneliness gives way to the sudden unexpected gift of love once more. And we endure. We endure.

177.

I realized something the other day. All my life, I've never really devoted myself to anything. Not that I haven't accomplished a lot. I have. I put myself through college. Raised a family. Worked hard. Paid all my bills...
But the truth is, I've never been one hundred percent committed to any of it. I slide through my days, doing the right thing, even if my mind or heart is a thousand miles away. I coast, and that seems good enough for most people. They don't even notice I'm not really here. All my life, I've never really devoted myself to anything. Never given it my all. And I wonder if I ever will?

178.

We can do this. You and me. Without being seen. Just in and out in ten minutes. It's easy.

I've got it all thought out. Been planning it for months. We go in, grab it and nobody'll ever know it was us. And just like that, our life changes.

One night, a little bit of courage, and we never have to worry about anything ever again.

We can do this. We can definitely do this.

179.

Okay. Get your taste buds ready and prepare to be amazed! You've never experienced anything like my homemade spaghetti and meatballs.

The secret is all in the sauce, and romantic Italians since the beginning of time understood that homemade sauce should be a truly sensuous experience.

It's not just the ingredients. It's the passion with which it all comes together. You smell and taste and savor hour after hour of subtle, simmering delight. Enveloping the kitchen with that unique, irresistible aroma of sautéed garlic, sweet onion and fresh basil. Gently digging your fingers into the warm meatball mix. Shaping and caressing each one with affection and tenderness. Doting over them as they learn to sizzle in a gentle bath of virgin olive oil. It's enough to take your breath away...

To Italians, food is love, and preparation is the foreplay. Taste this, and you'll understand...

180.

You don't have to say it. I can see it in your eyes. The pity. The disgust. It's so easy for you to judge me, isn't it? So easy for you to see me as vain and shallow. So easy to feel superior. But I want you to know it's not about vanity. It's about survival.

You know that story about the ugly duckling? That was me. The awkward child that no one ever noticed. The girl that never got asked out on a date. Never got invited to parties. Never given a second look...

And then one day, everything changed. I woke up. Looked in the mirror, and somehow, for some reason, I just didn't seem as ugly or awkward anymore. After an entire adolescence of invisibility and humiliation, I began to be noticed for the first time. The same people who teased me or ignored me all those years, suddenly invited me to parties. Asked me out on dates. Overnight, I became someone that somebody wanted. Somebody desired. And I got down on my knees and thanked heavens for finally turning me into a swan.

But they never tell you the rest of the story. That the magic doesn't last. That over the decades, the swan slowly changes back. Only now, it's twice as sad, because I've seen what it's like to be noticed. Felt what it's like to be desired. And I can't go back to being an ugly duckling again. So, I don't care if this is my fifth surgery or my fiftieth. You nip, tuck and stretch whatever you have to. Because I need at least one more year. One more year to be a swan again...

Comedic Monologues

181.

Do you believe in past lives? You know, how you used to be someone else, and then got reincarnated and came back as you this time? Well, I do. In fact, I know it's true. I went to this fortune teller yesterday. Madame Mysteria down on Seventh Street. And she told me I've had like a dozen past lives. I helped build the pyramids in Egypt. Then I was a medieval knight, you know with all the armor and stuff. Some lives I was a man, sometimes I came back as a woman. I guess you can do that with reincarnation. Sounds kind of freaky to me, but what do I know? Anyway, Madame Mysteria even told me I used to be a lumberjack, Catherine the Great, the Mona Lisa and Teddy Roosevelt! How cool is that? I was a president of the United States, a Russian Tsar, and the most famous painting in the world. People have been looking at my face for like five hundred years! Madame Mysteria said I'm not that famous yet in this life, but I will be real soon. All I have to do is figure out my true destiny. And she says she can tell me how if I pay her another fifteen hundred dollars.

So, can I borrow some money? As a former president, you know I'm good for it.

182.

Well, your honor, it's like this. I don't think Bubba really meant to blow off his eyebrows, run naked down the street and set his pick-up on fire. He loved that truck. Loved it more than life itself. Maybe not as much as he loved Jack Daniels, but that Ford F-150 meant a whole lot to him. That's why he insisted on deep fryin' a big ol' turkey in the bed of that four-by-four every Thanksgiving. I guess I should'a knowed things were gonna head south when that lightning storm hit, and Bubba just cranked up the Leonard Skynard to drown out the thunder. There he was, swiggin' down a fifth of Jack, clog dancin' to Sweet Home Alabama, and laughin' at all that rain coming down in slippery sheets. But who would'a known that big old lightning bolt would hit right smack in that truck bed, just at the split-second he tossed that eighteen-pound turkey into the deep fryer? I mean, that kinda thing don't happen every day.

Now I don't know if the deep fryer exploding caught Bubba's pants on fire, or if the lightning hit the boom box, which set off the three extra gasoline cans he forgot to take outa the truck. Either way, that fireball sure was somethin' to see, and turkey wasn't the only fried meat that day, I tell you!

But I do think Bubba learned his lesson about drinkin' and truck cookin' in tornado weather.

When I saw him in the hospital, he swore we're all doing next Thanksgiving at Cracker Barrel instead.

183.

Okay, Sweetheart. One bedtime story, then you have to go right to sleep.

Let me see...last night I told you about how Cinderella married the handsome Prince and lived happily ever after. But there's more to the story. You see, even though Cinderella thought she had found her Prince Charming, it didn't take long before he began to take her for granted. Dropping his dirty clothes all around the castle, expecting Cinderella to pick up after him. Leaving whiskers and nose hairs in the bathroom sink. Just like your Daddy does. And it didn't matter what was happening in the kingdom if there was a ball game on TV. Yes, just like Daddy. Even after the clock struck twelve, and all poor, tired Cinderella wanted to do was fall fast asleep, that totally oblivious Prince would scoot on over to her side of the bed with some less than Charming remark, like "whatta ya say, huh?" or "C'mon, Cindy. It's been three weeks!" It got so bad, Cinderella even considered asking her Fairy Godmother to turn that pushy Prince into a pumpkin, just so she could play Sleeping Beauty for a week or two.

So, the moral of the story is...men are pigs, even if they claim to be Charming. And the glass slipper is always half empty when it comes to the 'happily ever after' part. Now be a good girl and go to sleep.

I have to go pick up after your Daddy...

184.

My fellow Americans, in these troubled times, we simply cannot afford the bizarre and irresponsible policies of my opponent in this race. Now I am not saying my opponent is some kind of incompetent, insincere, feeble-minded crook… but let's be honest here…the man is about as straight as a barbed-wire slinky. All throughout this campaign, I have vowed to take the high road whenever possible. However, my opponent's greedy, unconscionable, special-interest-pandering behavior has turned every road into a toll road. So if you like your politics dirty and our public trust transformed into a dank and fetid sewer of corruption… if you prefer some arrogant plutocrat to look down on you with drooling distaste… if you want an irrational, dishonest, perverted thief shoving his itchy-twitchy, money-grubbing fingers into your pants pocket…then by all means, pull that lever for my totally undeserving opponent! On the other hand, if you desire a more gentlemanly and respectful public servant on your side, then I humbly ask for your vote.

185.

So, I was just sitting there and - BAM! – Just like that I get this great idea. No, better than a great idea…it was the perfect inspiration. Like some guardian angel of creativity just whopped me on the side of the head and said, "Hey! Stupid! Why not do it this way? "
And it worked. It really worked!

186.

I'm going to ask this once, and that's it. You got one
chance to tell me the truth. You blow it, or try some cute
and clever dance, and I'm outa here. And you got to live
with the consequences. You hear what I'm saying? Am I
being obtuse in anyway? Good. Because this is the most
important thirty seconds of your life, and I suggest you
think real hard about that before you open your mouth.
Okay. Just this one question. Yes or no. Was it you, who
took my leftover dessert out of the refrigerator?!

187.

Will it ever STOP SNOWING???!!
I can't remember the last time I saw the sun, or could
walk outside without my toes freezing off and my nose
dripping straight into my scarf.
HUMAN BEINGS ARE NOT MEANT TO LIVE
LIKE THIS! Trapped inside for months on end, waiting
for global warming to kick in. There are only so many
games of solitaire I can play on my iPhone. Only so
many times I can binge watch The Walking Dead, before
I feel like I'm one of them.
Last night, I found myself complaining about the weather
to my leftover broccoli. Yes, I am now at the point that I
am TALKING TO BROCCOLI! What's next?
Massaging the mashed potatoes?
I need sun. I need warmth. I need Spring.
And I need it NOW!

188.

My husband told me that he didn't find me stimulating enough. So, you know what I did? I went down to the local K-Mart and bought a whole cartload of makeup. Then I went home, took a long, luxurious bath. Did my hair all up and fancy. Slipped into a real sexy nightgown. Turned the lights down low, put on some soft music. Then slipped into the garage and grabbed two truck batteries, a set of jumper cables and electrified the toilet seat before he got home. I'll tell you what… he was stimulated that night! He was so stimulated, all his hair from the waist down caught fire. Boy, did I have fun putting that out…with spray-on bleach and a tennis racket. Served him right.

189.

Okay, screw your ears on tight and listen up, stupid. Just 'cause I smile and act all cheerful-like, don't mean I'm no empty-headed, brain-dead, happy robot-type. I had me my share of trouble, and my share of crazy like everybody else. And no, it ain't all red roses and lottery jackpots in my neck of the woods, believe you me. I seen some things that'd melt the corneas right off your eyeballs. That's how harsh my life's been. But no matter what, I chose to look the other way. Focus on the bright side. Slap on this happy face despite whatever crapstorm is rainin' down on me. So, you go ahead and think what you want, but, dammit, I intend to be cheerful! Y'hear?

190.

Tell me again how cute you think I am. How sweet and funny and charming you said I was. Like how you said I was so exciting and perfect. Your most romantic dream come true. Tell me again how adorable and sexy I am. And how you never met anyone who could turn you on with just a smile. And how you could die happy, if I would just come down from heaven to kiss you. And tell me again how warm and happy and content your life would be, if I would only be gracious enough to go out on even one date with you. How nothing that happened in your past, or would ever happen in your future, could match the magic of that very first moment when I would say "Let's grab some pizza." Talk to me like that…

191.

The name's Dirk Sludge, Private Investigator. Poker and prodder of the soft criminal underbelly in this town they call the River City. You may think it's all giggles and glamour sniffing the dirty laundry of people with a filthy past, but let me tell ya… It's hard work, long hours, bad food, tawdry women, Tuesday morning hangovers, and threatening letters from every collection agency and loan company in town.
If all that sounds good to you, come look me up. I'm listed in the phone book under hard luck…
That's me, Dirk Sludge. Private Eye…

192.

I'd like to talk for a moment about a sensitive issue
facing our community… The overpopulation of a certain
sub-species that threatens our environment and our
society as a whole.

It has become clear that America is becoming overrun by
a flood of friendly but useless creatures. Whole families
may go hungry while these unproductive species are
overfed and pampered. In any supermarket, the aisle
space devoted to baby food is half as large as the displays
of specialty foods for these common parasites. It is a sure
symbol of the decline of our civilization. Of course, they
are living things, and for that reason we should consider
extermination only as a last resort. Yet, determined
efforts must be made to slow their alarming rate of
multiplication.

That is why STSNA was formed.

The Society to Spay and Neuter Attorneys.

With the growing number of lawyers, law students and
paralegals, our society is in danger of becoming
overwhelmed by frivolous lawsuits, corporate bickering,
and fraudulent bankruptcies. The only solution is
enforced sterilization to allow more productive species to
grow in our societies.

If you have a lawyer, or know someone who has a
lawyer, do your part. Send them down to our center for a
quick and almost painless operation.

This public service announcement has been paid for by
STSNA…the Society to Spay and Neuter Attorneys.

193.

Ahhh... This is the life! It's the perfect spot for our honeymoon. Pristine sand. Warm sun. Palm trees. The sensuous rhythm of the waves crashing onto the beach. Hot girls in bikinis walking by and...uh, not that I noticed any of those hot girls. Women. People in bikinis. Female people, I mean, in um, any bathing-type garment they happen to be wearing on their bodies. And by hot, I meant in terms of temperature, and not the soft, firm curves of their...uh, people-shapes in general. Because I don't notice things like that! No way! I'm a married man now, with the most perfect woman in the world lying next to me. And I'd be crazy to notice something like that...oh, my god...unbelievable purple bikini over there...Which I am definitely NOT seeing, because I am one hundred percent focused on my pretty wife, who... YEOW! Just poured ice-cold Dr. Pepper right in my lap. Wow, paradise is a lot chillier than I thought it would be.

194.

So, he turns to her and says... "I wouldn't brag about those if I were you!" And man, you should have seen her face! She turned this bright red and couldn't say another word. He laughed so hard, he fell off his chair. The rest of us started busting out, too. Man, it was classic. The perfect put-down line.
Of course, she filed for divorce the next day, which was kind of a shame. But you have to admit, it was still pretty funny...

195.

I didn't want to say anything, but if you really must know… There are one or two things you do that might possibly be considered…somewhat less than endearing. Well…since you asked. I used to think it was cute the way you licked the plate after a spaghetti dinner. I'm not finding it as cute anymore. And passing gas in church, then getting all giggly over the way people sitting all around you pretend not to notice is fine when you're ten or twelve maybe, but it's the reason even our close friends won't sit next to us on Sunday anymore. Of course, that doesn't mean you aren't absolutely perfect in every other way! Really, I couldn't ask for someone who is kinder, more thoughtful and… Okay, if you really want to know…that squeaky smacking noise you make when you suck your teeth sounds like someone dropkicking a canary. So, if you could stop doing it maybe twelve or fifty times an hour, I would really, *really* appreciate it. Oh, and things like toothpaste and clean underwear are not just for special occasions. Okay?

196.

This is the best thing I've ever tasted. I mean it. This is incredible. I never knew you could cook like this. I mean it just melts in your mouth. And that taste, unbelievable. You've got to tell me what's in it. What's your secret ingredient? Uh…you're kidding, right? No, really… *That's* what I'm eating? Uh, excuse me for a moment… I think I 'm gonna be sick....

197.

Whadda you mean cowboys don't pray? What kind of darn fool nonsense is that? I tell you what, you get yourself up on the back of a big ol' rodeo bull, that's kickin' and buckin,' and a darn-sight madder 'n any mother-in-law not invited for Thanksgiving dinner. You fly outta that chute, holdin' on for dear life, while twelve-hundred pounds of nothin' but ornery, tries to rattle your teeth through your rib cage. Then you look up and see only ground rushin' at you, 'cuz you're flyin' through the air upside down, and that ton-and-a-quarter of USDA prime beef is hoofin' back your way, lookin' to return the favor for those spurs you dug in his sides. And just before what's left of your face hits that dirt hard, and his hooves commence to dancin' on your skull, at that moment, you learn to pray real fast. And you best be hoping that God's on your side, and that there bull ain't a better Christian than you, I tell you what.

198.

Okay. I know I look good. Really good. In fact, it's almost embarrassing how good I look. Yeah, I know everyone says you're supposed to be modest and all that… but maybe modesty is just an excuse for those people who don't look as good as I do… I mean, you can't expect me to apologize for being this hot.
After all, if God blessed me with looks like this, the least I can do is let others appreciate them, don't you think?

199.

There is something I need to tell you. Something I should have mentioned a long time ago. I...I just don't know how to say it. You know how much I love you, and that you and I are like the perfect couple. We love the same movies. The same restaurants. Even the same jokes. I love how you spontaneously rub my shoulders when I'm stressed, without my even having to ask you to. And how you let me vent every time my tool of a boss pulls some tool-like move at work. And you listen. You really listen. And you know I think you are the sexiest guy ever. Which is why this is so hard for me to say... You are a bad kisser. I'm talking really squish face, remedial level kissing. I can't even figure out what it is you do with your lips and drool that makes it so freakishly icky. And that's even before we get to the tongues, and then it's... Huh? What do you mean, *I'm* a bad kisser too? That is so false! I'll have you know these lips are legendary. It's a fact!

200.

I don't know why parents think grades are so important. I never heard anybody say George Washington really messed up on his spelling test, so we shouldn't make him president. I don't think anybody cares how Abraham Lincoln did in math. I bet Shakespeare was really bad in gym, but they still make us read his plays. Anyway, that's what 'm going to tell my parents when they see my report card. Maybe they won't get as mad.

201.

So, there I am, working out on the treadmill, when *HE* walks in... Tall, curly hair, and the most perfect body you've ever seen. He's like one of those Greek sculptures, every muscle chiseled in perfect he-man proportions. Pecs stretching his tank top and leg muscles flexing as he walks. Every woman in the place nearly falls off our treadmills, he so perfect.

And there I am, trying not to stare, as he starts working out. This glassy shimmer of sweat making his statue-like body look even sexier. The treadmill says my heart rate is now one-sixty and climbing, even though I'm not moving, or even breathing.

Then this beautiful man, this Greek god, moves to a weight machine and sets it for three-fifty. More than any other guy in the place can press. He takes one big gulp of air... Grabs the bar in his big, sensuous hands... Starts to lift... And then lets out this absolutely enormous fart! It's so loud, it echoes through my headphones. And suddenly this perfectly sculpted man isn't a Greek god anymore. He's just another fallible, gas-filled human being, like my husband at home.

Everyone in the place starts laughing, and Mr. Way-Too-Perfect gets so embarrassed, he runs straight out of the gym, and we never saw him again.

So, when I got home, I hugged my husband, and realized that, even if he's not perfectly sculpted, he's the perfect man for me.

202.

I want to trust you. I really do. I know you want to be someone I can depend on. And I know you will try really hard to be reliable and responsible. It's just that… well, you're a man, and we all know how men are. You talk a good game, but can I really count on you to get me what I need? It's not like I'm even asking for a lot. Just a few simple things. That's all I need. But the second I let you out that door, you forget everything, and go pick up the first thing that catches your eye. Don't deny it. You remember last week? And the week before? You came home, looking guilty. Bringing who knows what into my house! But not this time. I am going to make a list, and you are going to march down to that supermarket and buy exactly what I ask for. Milk, eggs and brown sugar. Take the list so you don't forget and buy something crazy. No beer, Cheetos or WD-40. Just milk, eggs and brown sugar. Can I trust you this time?

203.

There's no easy way to say it… I'm done. I'm over. I've had it with you. You can't have a relationship with someone who doesn't care enough to pay any attention to simplest thing. Someone who can't take five minutes from her favorite TV show to listen to what I have to say. I'm tired of having conversations with myself. I'm not asking for a lot here. Just someone who cares enough to… Yes, I am talking to you… I said, there's no easy way to say it… I'm done. I'm over. I've had it with you…

204.

How could you?! I never know you could be this cruel.
What were you thinking, huh?! Today's our anniversary,
and I go all out to to dress up and look my best for you.
Then you take me to an All-You-Can-Eat Buffet!
Now look at me! I'm thirty-seven pounds heavier than
when I walked in two hours ago! You know what I'm
like. You knew exactly what would happen! I'm so
stuffed, I look like a Thanksgiving turkey. I lost my waist
around my third helping of fried chicken, candied
meatloaf and Cajun mac and cheese. I had so many
romantic plans for tonight, now all I'll be able to do is
burp, groan and waddle. You ruined our anniversary,
and… Wait a minute. Aren't you going to eat that last
bite of cheesecake? It'd be a shame to waste it...

205.

What's the big deal about cheerleaders anyway? I mean,
they have those silly uniforms and those stupid cheers
that don't even rhyme. But all the boys in school fall all
over themselves just to sit with them in the cafeteria or
take them to prom. Don't they know that there's a lot
more to girls than pompoms and fake smiles?
Real women have depth, and intelligence and…
What? I made the squad?! Awesome!
Go Team! Give me a T...!
Give me an E! Give me an A!

206.

Aren't you the cute one?! Aren't you just a sweetie pie?!
Look at your beautiful widdle face. You want me to
scratch behind your ears? You like that don't you? What
a good boy you are! Yes, you are. A very good boy. So
smart and cute and cuddly! You want a treat, huh? Ah!
No drooling! You know the rules. You don't get a treat if
you drool. It's hard enough to keep this house clean
without you drooling all over the place. Oh, don't give
me those sad, puppy dog eyes. You know I love you.
And you know I can't resist that widdle face. Let's go out
and you can have a treat when we get back in. Okay?
Doesn't that sound yummy? Oh, and you should go
fetch the dog. He probably has to go outside, too. What
a good boy you are! A very good boy!

207.

You know what? I'm ready to go a little wild. I owe it to
myself. You see, I've been the good girl all my life.
Always did the right things, at the right time, for all the
right people. Never got into any trouble. Studied, while
all the other kids went out to party. Worked hard. Got a
good career. Became the perfect wife. Dedicated Mom.
Dependable friend and respectable neighbor. So yeah, I
am way overdue for a rampage. And tonight, I'm
throwing off that good girl rep and going full-out, old
school crazy!
So, tell me, what does a Margarita taste like? Hope it's
non-fat. And it doesn't have any alcohol in it, right?

208.

Cute? Check…. Smart? Sort of… Sexy? Oh my God! And you told me this dating site would be a waste of time. But look, she is the perfect woman. Well, maybe not perfect, with her criminal record and removable teeth. But a real catch. And talk about friendly! I mean, she'd have to be, to be a greeter at Walmart, wouldn't she? Well, before they fired her for wedging that man's head in the bas-cart. I'm sure he had it coming. I know she's ambitious, because she wanted to make sure I had a job and made at least six figures before she'd go out with me. So that's a plus. It means she won't date just anybody. She's discriminating, in the good sense of the word. Although I bet someone PhotoShopped those swastika tattoos to make her look bad. To keep her for themselves, you know? Disease-free? I guess she forgot to answer that one. Yup, I really think she could be the one. I knew *Desperate-4-Affection.com* would pay off!

209.

There was this one point when you and I were together. I was holding you so tightly, and you smiled up at me with that look of yours. And then I got lost in your eyes. The way they sparkled with warmth and tenderness… and I stopped. Everything I was trying to say was gone. I just sat there, holding you, realizing this was exactly what I want to do for the rest of my life. What I need to do every day. Every second… But then you sneezed like right in my face, and that moment was so over!

210.

You've got to be kidding me.
You show up outta nowhere… standing at my door looking that hot and that innocent…and then expect me to act like nothing's wrong? Like nothing ever happened? Did you think I'd forget the thirty-five hundred dollars that just happened to disappear from my bank account the day you left? Or all those 'mysterious' charges on my credit card? Or all those calls at two in the morning from friends of yours who would never leave their name? What do you think I am? Stupid? …
Oh, I see… Why didn't you tell me you were working an undercover case? National security, huh? Need to know basis? Okay, I understand. I'm not stupid, you know…

211.

Let me tell ya, them politicians ain't nothin' but a bunch of damn crooks. Ever' single one of 'em is just scratchin' and sniffin' around fer ever' hard-earned dollar of mine they can get their dirty little paws on. Ain't no real demokercy anymore. I tell you what…ol' George Wash'ntin, would be spinnin' an' spittin' in his grave, if he saw the kind of no-sense bozos been runnin' the governmint these days. But one o' these days, all us ever'day good ol' boys is gonna rise up and give 'em what for. We gonna take this here country back…and mebbe give the ol' USA a lil' common sense again.
Lord knows, they could use it.

212.

Wow. I can't believe like we texted and Facebooked, and Snap Chatted and talked on the phone like forever, and all that time you never told me that before. I mean you were like my dream date, secret crush and best friend all rolled into one, and the absolutely sweetest funniest person in the world. And now you go and tell me you're a Scorpio? I don't do Scorpios! I mean, everybody who has ever seriously messed up my life was a Scorpio. Boyfriends, bosses, friends who turned out to be jerks. Rude waiters, mean teachers and strangers who steal your parking space. All Scorpios! That's why I don't do Scorpios. I can't even talk to you anymore, you…you, November-birth guy! I just wish you had told me that before I bought my wedding dress…

213.

I've got to tell you…the people in my family are just…I don't know. Crazed. Insane. From another planet. My mom is always singing, like everything in the world makes her happy. And my dad, he's one of those people who never met a stranger. He'll go right up and talk to anyone. And in five minutes, it's like they're his best friend. He'll be laughing and slapping them on the back like they grew up together. It's weird, I tell you. Why can't I have a normal family, like on reality TV?

214.

Last night I had a revelation! That big idea I've been
searching for my whole life.

I was lying in bed with all these crazy thoughts buzzing
around my head, and then POW! There it was! The
answer to everything. The idea that was going to make
me rich. Give my life purpose. And not just me. This was
going to change the world! Make everyone's life better.
Solve the energy crisis. Protect the environment. End
world hunger. Maybe even eliminate the need for war!
Okay, that may be reaching, but I tell you, this is big.
Awesomely hugely big!

So, I laid there in the dark for like hours, fleshing out all
the details. It was all so clear to me now. And I knew I
had to write it down, or history and mankind would
never forgive me.

Fortunately, I keep a notebook by my bed, so I shook
the drowsiness off and wrote down my big idea before I
lost it, you know? And only after I committed this epic
brainstorm to paper, would I let myself drift happily off
into the most peaceful, contented sleep I've ever known.
Anyway, I had to rush right over this morning and read
you what I wrote down… "The geological square of
purple doesn't play nice with wind powered duck
robots."…

I guess I wasn't as awake as I thought I was.

It made a lot of sense last night…

215.

Look, I don't know what you're getting upset about.
How could I know Wanda was going to be at that party?
I mean, it's been five whole years. And who expected her
to show up in a dress like that? I mean the way it clung to
her body like some kinda sexy snake about to shed its
skin...

Uh, not that you wouldn't have been just as much a
snake in that dress. Well, not a snake, but... hell, you
know what I mean...

I told you a hundred times, Wanda and I are ancient
history. I haven't thought about her in a couple of wee...
uh, *years*. A couple of years! Believe me, she means as
little to me as that stupid painting over there!

Oh, that's right... You bought me that painting on our
anniversary. Well... What I meant to say was, she means
less to me than that stupid... uh, that wonderfully
expressive piece of modern art mounted on the wall. The
whole night, did you see me once try to mount her?

Um, bad choice of words...

Listen, sweetheart. You're the only woman in my life.
You are my heart and my soul. The lady who puts a smile
on my lips and the fire in these hips. You don't ever have
to Wanda what I'm thinking.

I mean *wonder* what I'm thinking! Wonder!

I'm sleeping on the couch tonight, aren't I, sweetheart?

216.

Oh my god! Are his lips still moving? I don't even know
how long he's been talking at me. I lost track after the
first twenty minutes of his dog's colonoscopy story. I
mean, I like animals and everything, but after all those
doggie doodoo details, I just wanted to scream, "Krazy
Glue the mutt's butt shut!"
And okay, I get it. You got chest hair. It doesn't mean
you have to unbutton your shirt down to your belly
button. This is a blind date, not an audition for the next
Planet of the Apes sequel. I keep waiting for you to shed
one or two of those chestie curls into your beer mug. If
you were going to go with the 'gorilla chic' motif, you
should've ordered a 'Fuzzy Navel.'
OMG, he is STILL…TALKING…! This is officially the
Worst Date Ever.

217.

Cut that out! You know that when you slide me one of
those not-so-innocent little smiles…or you casually drop
one of your slightly suggestive comments… my brain
screeches to a stop in mid-sentence. It doesn't matter
what we are talking about, or how knowledgeable or
excited I am about the subject. You start teasing me and
my mind turns to mush and I…um, I…uh…There you
go again! That playful little smile. I don't know why you
have this power over me, but it's evil. Pure evil. So, cut
that out and come kiss me, before I make an even bigger
fool of myself!

218.

You should'a been there. The boss walks in and shouts in that red-faced, huffy-obnoxious voice of his... *"If I find out who filled my briefcase with pudding, they're fired!!"* Well, Luanda and I nearly fall off our chairs, we're trying so hard not to laugh. I mean, here he is, eyes bulging out. Sweat running out from under his two-dollar toupee... and one sleeve of his suit, brown to the elbow with chocolate pudding. I mean, it really wasn't funny, but man...you should have seen his face!
Anyway, that's why I'm applying for this job today. And uh...I'm not sure I'll be able to get a recommendation from my last employer...

219.

Okay. First off, he was gorgeous. I mean, 'take your breath away' gorgeous. With these big, dark eyes and a silly, crooked smile that made me all wiggly, hot and tingly all over. He looked right at me, and he got me. I mean really got me. He knew exactly what I wanted. I didn't even have to say, 'paper or plastic,' because he knew the kind of woman I was and what I needed right then and there. And when he grabbed that gallon of milk in his wide, sensuous hands...his biceps flexing from that Extra-Large box of Tide-with-Bleach, I let out a gasp that even the people way back in aisle three must have heard. And yes, I know I shouldn't go through Express Check Out with Twenty-eight items, but what can I do? I'm in love with the cute bagger in Lane Four?

220.

You touched me! I can't believe you just touched me like that! Don't deny it, I know what I felt. I was just standing there, and you brushed up against me in the most intimate and inappropriate manner!

I don't care if the bus was crowded and it was accidental. We are two complete and total strangers. And physical contact is something that should only happen after we have been properly introduced. Like after I tell you my name is Wanda June and you say your name is...? Okay, George Bartley. And then you say, it's nice to meet you, Wanda June and ask me a few polite, but not too personal questions about my job at the discount earring counter at the mall, and I ask you about your job as a...? Okay, as a dental appliance salesman. Which I imagine is pretty interesting work...

And maybe after that, we chat some more, and then meet for coffee, and maybe if we hit it off and are still really attracted to each other...only then would I invite you back to my place on North Chartreuse Avenue, right behind the Dairy Freeze, where we could chat quietly on my sofa, watching *Sleepless in Seattle* with Tom Hanks and Meg Ran, which is my favorite romantic movie and always makes me cry and smile at the end...and ONLY THEN would I even consider giving you permission to touch me like that!

So … have you ever seen *Sleepless in Seattle*?

221.

Here's the way I see it…
First off, you're stupid.
Secondly, it's all completely irrelevant and even if it wasn't, nobody cares anyhow. Or they wouldn't, if you didn't go and make such a big deal of it all.
And third… well, you're stupid again. I mean, Guinness Book of World Records stupid. Mega-ignorant. Dumber than a double cream doughnut on a diet menu.
It was only a little lie and a bit of creative bookkeeping. And it's not like the team didn't waste enough money on new uniforms anyway, when the old ones the kids were wearing for the last six years were perfectly good, and you could still read most of the writing on them from the first two rows.
But you had to go and point out my new Weber deluxe barbecue grill, right there in the middle of the parent's meeting. Like I couldn't have gone and bought that grill myself, even though Elliot's still out on disability and I got fired from the Dizzy Mart last month, when some other buttinski nosy loudmouth like you had the nerve to blame me when the register would never quite balance at the end of the night.
It's all nothing but stupid, and I'm the one who gets blamed for it.
Just my luck.

222.

I can't help it. I love women. I mean I *really* love them.
Love everything about them. Tall or short. Shy or
sophisticated. Wild child or church lady. I love 'em all.
The way they walk. The way their hair smells. The way
their noses crinkle when they smile. Those soft, huggable
curves. The long lashes and even longer legs. The way
they flirt, knowing what power they have over us. The
way words rush all bubbly fun from their mouths when
they're out with their girlfriends. And even the fact that
it's okay to be a girl and have girlfriends, when you'd
probably wallop anybody who said us boys were hanging
with our boyfriends. I love the way they shriek at spiders
and think baby animals are cute, even when they're
halfway to grandmaville. And what guy would say shoes
were 'adorable'? Women… I could watch them all day
long. 'Course my wife would up and kill me if I do…

223.

You. Yeah, you with the face! Where you think you're
goin', huh? You think you can just get up and run out on
us, like nobody's gonna notice? You think I'm that
dumb, huh? Well, let me tell you somethin'… nobody
walks out on Bernie the Blade! You join my crew, you
don't leave until someone digs your body outa some
cement walkway or…Oh…Well, it's over there down the
hall, and take a right. Next to the juke box.
But hey, don't take too long! Bernie the Blade don't like
to be kept waitin',' y'hear?

224.

Okay. You've got twenty seconds to kiss me and kiss me right. I always say that if you don't get that first kiss right. If you can't make the hair on the back of my neck stand up and my toes curl under in that very first kiss…well, then it probably is never gonna happen at all. So, no pressure, but if you have any chance with me, you better be real good at taking my breath away in the next twenty seconds. Because I don't give second chances to sloppy kissers and I…Okay…whoa… I have to say that was, uh… on a scale from one-to-ten, I'd have to give that a seventeen. At least a seventeen. And uh, wow… Definitely wow. So, are we on for next Friday?

225.

Let me tell you what love is. It's this strange and scary flutter in your chest whenever you see her eyes. And your breath catches when she suddenly turns and smiles at you. You can't help it, you go through the day grinning like an idiot, and before you know it, everything reminds you of her. It's like every song you hear was written about her. Every painting captures the gentle curves of her face. Every sunset just reminds you of how beautiful she would look in that soft, glowing light.
In other words. Love makes you stupid. A complete moron.
But hey, if we're lucky, we should all be that stupid someday.

226.

Why did I marry him? I really have no idea… He's rude, lazy. Dumb as a day-old doughnut. Has hair in places you don't even want to know about. And expels enough gas to heat half the homes in Los Angeles. I swear, that man thinks 'gaseous' is how you say thank you in Spanish. The thing is, aside from a few bad habits...okay, hundreds of bad habits... he's really good with the kids. Takes the time to play with them. Helps them with their homework and science projects. Tucks them in and tells them bedtime stories every night. He even makes up his own stories with each kid as the hero. The boys love it. Sometimes I watch their little eyes light up when he's weaving one of his stories. They lay there in the darkness, entranced by his words. Imagining all the magical possibilities of childhood... and I think to myself, maybe the rest isn't all that bad… Then he teaches them to fart out the alphabet and the spell is broken.

227.

I don't know. Really, I don't. Where do *you* think this relationship is going? Are we looking at forty or fifty years of happily ever after, or is this some kind of extended one-month stand?
Cause either way, it's okay with me. I can do whatever you want. I can be whatever you need me to be. Just let me know what my role is here, and I'm good.
Really, I'm good. Just let me know.

228.

I gotta say…I'm mad as a pit bull in a blender! You know what they did to me at work today? They promoted me! That's right, I was doin' just fine hiding out in my little cubicle. Answering a few phone calls, shuffling some papers and keeping up on the latest celebrity scandals on line. Then suddenly, my boss up and says he wants me to take over the whole warehouse division! Sure, it's more money, but it's also on my feet all day. No long lunches. No leaving early …and I actually have to talk to people! It just ain't fair!

229.

I have a confession to make…I have loved you my entire life. Even before we met, I knew you were out there. My twin. My soul mate. Someone who I knew intimately, and who knew me inside and out, from the very first moment our eyes met. The first time I saw you smile. The first time my fingers brushed your cheek. I dreamed about you, night after night, even though I may not have known exactly what you would look like. But I knew I could never be whole, never be happy, until I found you. Until you found me. Then all I had to do was give you my entire heart and all my love for the next fifty or sixty years. And that's all I expect from you in return. Anyway, I think this is going really well for a first date. Can I buy you an ice cream? You do like ice cream, don't you? That's kind of a deal breaker for me...

230.

Okay. I can either vote for this bill or vote against it. If I vote for it, they're all going to be mad at me. They'll say, 'what if it doesn't work as planned?' Not that it ever does. Or worse, what if it does work? Then they will expect that same level of efficiency in everything! And I'll never hear the end of it. So maybe I should vote no. There's plenty of reasons to vote against it. Or at least they tell me there are. I guess I should have read the damn thing first. But who has time these days? So maybe I better say yes. No, uh, no. Definitely a no. But then I'd have to explain *why* I voted no, which would be harder than just going along and hiding my yes vote with the majority. But what if it's close? What if my vote is the deciding factor? The one that pushes it over the top? Then everyone'll blame me if it doesn't work…or if it does! They all think it's so easy to be a senator. I knew I should have read that bill last night…

231.

Can you keep a secret? Because I can't. I mean I thought I could. I even promised I would when Jennie told it to me, but now it's like my head is bursting, I want to tell someone so bad. But I promised, so I won't. At least, I'll try not to. I mean, you can't expect someone to keep a secret forever, can you? Especially a really, really good one like this. That wouldn't be fair, would it?

232.

Excuse me... I'm sorry to interrupt your phone call.
But...did that just happen back there? That's okay tell
him to wait... I just have to know, because of the way you
were smiling at me... a few minutes ago... In the stands...
I was jumping up and down, screaming; "Defense, you
hopeless losers!" and you turned and gave me the
sweetest smile anyone's ever given me, and... Why don't
you just tell him you'll call back later... Anyway, I felt we
had sort of a moment back there, and... Look, tell him
we're making a connection here that may involve your
whole future with what could be the man of your dreams
and...No, I meant me. *I* could be the man of your
dreams... and well, if he can't handle it, then just hang
up, so we can get back to... hey, where are you going? I
didn't even tell you my name yet...Hey, come back! We
have a connection here!

233.

Do you like coffee? I like coffee. No, actually, I love
coffee. Really love it. Really, really love it. Joe, Java,
Ground Goodness, Fresh Brewed Ecstasy and Black
Delight. Coffee starts my day and makes life worth living.
But not just any coffee. No decaf, day-old, Grandma's
cheap bean sludge drippings for me. I need the good
stuff. Crave it. The rich, imported, five-bucks-for-a-
cardboard-cup – steaming jolt of heaven. The smell, the
taste, the get-me-off-my-butt-and-out-the-door kick in
the morning. So, you want a cup? I'm buying!

234.

I had a dream the other night. One of those failure dreams I usually get. Where everything is going wrong. But in this dream, I finally got my big chance. A major part in a smash hit on Broadway. It was everything I worked so hard for all these years. My name in lights. Everyone I know in the audience.

So, there I am. On Broadway… The curtain goes up… and suddenly I realize I don't know the script! Had never read it. Not even sure who may character is, or what I should be doing! But there I was in front of thousands of people. All my friends and family. All the big names in the industry… and I don't know any of my lines!

Jennifer Lawrence throws me my cue and I just stand there. Stand there on that huge, brightly lit stage with my mouth open and absolutely nothing coming out. I'm just standing there, looking stupid. And all this time is going by, and Jennifer Lawrence is glaring at me, like she's gonna kill me for making her look bad too.

Then the audience starts to laugh. And then boo. Some get up and start to walk out. And all this time I'm standing there in the spotlight, I can't think of anything to say at all. Not a word…

Finally, Jennifer runs up and punches me square in the nose. She accuses me of ruining her career, then kicks me in the crotch, really hard, and that hurts so bad I wake up immediately.

I really hate that dream.

It's the third time I've had it this week…

235.

Yeah, I admit. I did notice you. Okay, I did more than notice. I was watching you watching me and thinking...is she interested? Is she infatuated? Or do I have something on my nose? Or some food stuck in my teeth? I'm glad I didn't, because I really wanted to make an impression on you. A good impression. A heavy-breathing, tingling-in-your-chest, can't-hide-your-smile-type impression. I want you to think what it would be like if our lips touched... accidentally at first, and then again and again, until your knees weaken, and you can't think of anyone but me for the rest of your life and... oh, uh, is this your husband? Maybe I should bring the check now. And um, by the way...your desserts are on the house...

236.

I am going to take over the company one day. I have my five-year plan and my ten-year plan. I'll start quietly; developing skills, making contacts, amassing resources, and determining my best means of attack. I'll see who I can work with, and who needs to go. Because when I take over, I plan to run a tight ship. Efficiency is my way of doing business. And if you are not with me, you're against me. So, it might be a good time to let me know where you stand. Yes, sir. I know it's only my third day on the job. And, yes, I am aware this is an entry level position. But I wanted you to know that I don't plan to be in the mail room forever. I am going to take over the company one day. You can count on it.

237.

I love your laugh. All of them. The giggles you can't control. Your little chuckle that sounds almost nasty, when it's totally innocent. And that sudden explosion of laughter that sounds so sweet, it's impossible to resist. Before I know it, I'm holding my sides and laughing with you, even when I don't know what we're laughing about. I just never met anyone who could be so overtaken by joy. You get this mischievous little sparkle in your eyes, and a grin that's so cute and contagious, I'm smiling too. And then the giggles start. The laughter builds and spills out of you until I want to hug you and kiss your smiling face and thank you for saving me from a life without you. Without your laugh. Okay, so I get carried away, but you can stop laughing now. No, really. It wasn't that funny.

238.

I know this may sound a little crazy, but hear me out. What if there is life on other planets. And what if they look exactly like us, came down to our planet, and maybe have been here so long they forgot, like, that they're even aliens and everything. And what if...really, what if the only way we can tell who they are is that they're a lot more clumsy than us, because they have less gravity and everything on their own planet, so they'd trip over their heavier legs here on Earth. And what if that's why that weird girlfriend of yours can't dance? Huh?

239.

I can't wait 'til I grow up. Being a kid is no fun at all.
Adults are always telling you what to do, and where to
go, and when to do your homework. They complain
about what I watch on TV, or the music I listen to. It's
always do this, do that, or don't ever do that! Like I said,
it's no fun at all…

Of course, it's seriously cool that I don't have to go to
work all day, like my dad does. Or pay the bills, like my
Mom does. And I'd really hate to cook dinner every day
and have to pick up after my little sister all the time…

Well, maybe I'll stay a kid a little longer…

240.

I really thought my sister had the perfect marriage. I used
to tell all my friends, "That's what I want it to be like
when I get married." They seemed to have it so easy. I
mean, they had fun doing things together. They laughed
all the time. And they couldn't take their eyes off each
other. I'd watch them, when they didn't know I was
looking. Katy would be across the room, talking or doing
something silly…and Chad would be just sitting back and
smiling at her with so much love in his eyes. She didn't
see it, but I did. And that's what I want. Someone to look
at me like that, even when I'm not looking at him.

So, tell me about your brother.

Is he cute?

241.

Mmmmm. Admit it. There is nothing sexier than two people cooking together. Letting someone you barely know into your private kitchen can be so…intimate. Two people moving as one. Creating together. Each revealing their deep down, secret recipes. A pinch of this. A touch of that. A hint of adventure. The heat of the stove. The pleasing scent of unfamiliar spices. The gentle coaxing of ingredients over a rising flame. A little hot oil. A sudden sizzle. A gasp of delight. Building to a climax of culinary passion in one overpoweringly pleasing dish. Mmmmm. Unless you want to go out. I have Taco Bell coupons.

242.

I need this deal. You can't take it away from me. I've worked too long and too hard on this. I've given up nights with my family and any semblance of a normal life to chase this down. And now when it's so close I can almost taste it… you want to give it to Carter? Carter who doesn't know the first thing about what it took to get it this far. To get it this close. Listen. The truth is… I go under without this deal. I'm serious. I lose the house. My wife leaves me. And you know I'll become the laughingstock of this office if Carter gets to reap all the rewards for my work. What I'm trying to say is… I know you're the boss and I know you have the right to make whatever decisions you want…but damn it, you can't take this away from me! You can't be that stupid! What do you mean I'm fired…?

243.

Yeah, it's a setback. More than a setback. It's another kick to the chest with a stiletto heel through the left lung, with my dreams leakin' out my ears like a meltdown at a nuclear power plant kind of setback.

Once again, the world chooses to treat me like I'm the only living crash test dummy, with another six hundred high impact face-plants to go on my contract.

I'm so tired of being that video game zombie, who gets his head blown off in Level One, when all I'm tryin' to do is munch a little brain matter, you know?

Okay, bad analogy, but I'm asking myself, when is it enough? When will the universe finally decide I've paid more than my share of dues, and throw me a break?

I could really use one right about now.

But don't you think I'm giving up. Not me. Failure is not an option. I'm like Rocky, heading into the twelfth bloody round, still leading with my face.

And you know why? Because I'm Marv Botanski, that's why! Marv Friggin' Botanski, and next time, I take that driver's test, I am gonna stop at every red light, and let every little old lady make it all the way across the street before I hit the gas.

Sixth time's a charm. And my new license is gonna read 'Marv Friggin' Botanski.'

That's a promise!

244.

I don't know what you want from me. What you expect
me to say. If we are being totally honest here...I don't
know what *I* expect me to do... I started out with so
many plans. I knew exactly how everything was supposed
to go tonight. What I was supposed to say. How I was
supposed to behave in a place like this, and then... well,
then, there you were...staring down at me with those
dark, dreamy eyes. And suddenly...suddenly every
thought flew right out of my head, and here I sit, all
tongue-tied and shy. Like every single thing has become
all slow motion and wobbly, but in a good way, you
know? And second after second is marked by my
pounding heart...so loud, I'm afraid everybody sitting
around me can hear it too. You're waiting for me to say
something, and I realize I haven't even taken a single
breath ever since you asked me. Asked me what I
wanted. I know I better answer soon, or you'll just walk
away, maybe to talk to someone else. Like that blonde at
that table over there. I...I can't let you do that. I can't let
you walk away without an answer. Without telling you
what I really want. It'd ruin everything.
So, okay. Here goes...What do I want?
Ummm... I guess I'll start with the shrimp cocktail
appetizer, and then maybe the steak or the fish. Or
maybe the chicken, or even the pasta...
Oh, I don't know...what do you recommend, dreamy
eyes?

245.

I'm not talking to you. I've got nothing to say and absolutely no one to say it to. And you can't make me say anything either. I know that's what you're thinking, like you have this amazing, mystical, sexual power over me, and that no matter what I say, or don't say, you can always get me to do exactly what you want. But those days are over. They're over as of right now! Because I'm not talking to you, and you can't make me. No way. I'm not saying a word. Lips locked. Mouth sealed tight as if I swallowed Krazy Glue. Don't expect me to say a single word. Not one. Not me.

Because even if you wanted me to tell you what was bothering me, I wouldn't. There's just too much to say. I mean, I could go on and on about the way your eyes scooped up that room. The way you flirted with everyone at the party, as if I wasn't even there. But I won't say anything like that. Uh uh. No way, Jose. I'm through talking. I'm not going to speak to you or say anything at all. Because even if I did, it wouldn't do much good. And besides, I'm not talking to you. That's just the way it is. You might as well go chatter up all those other bimbos you were drooling all over, because you are not going to get an answer out of me. No way, no how. I am keeping my feelings to myself. Silent as a statue. Locked tight as a drum. That's just the way it is. Because I'm not talking to you.

Deal with it.

246.

Why am I even here? Can you tell me that? I could be
out courting voters in one of those big states, like
California or New York. States that really count. Instead,
I have to waste my time in these one-horse towns, with
Gomer the Governor over there, and the Mayor of
Mayberry. These guys probably think 'Senate' is
something you say when you drop a letter in the mailbox.
"It's okay! I jus' sen'– it!" But here I am eating greasy
food. Shaking greasy hands. Where the babies have more
teeth than the adults. So, let's just get this pitiful excuse
for a rally over with, so I can…Uh…what do you mean,
the microphone is on…? I…uh…What I meant to say is
that I *love* the good people of this state! You are the heart
and soul of America! And when I am elected President…

247.

It's been two months and I can still feel your hand in
mine. That warm, soft touch. The way your fingers
wrapped around mine, like they were meant to be there
from the moment we were first born… And the way you
moved your thumb gently over my palm. Slowly, like you
were exploring…or maybe even afraid. Or you were
trying to memorize the feeling for the rest of your life.
One touch of your hand, and I haven't been able to sleep
without thinking about that moment, over and over
again…
Can you imagine what kind of shape I'd be in if we had
actually kissed?

248.

I knew I shouldn't have gotten out of bed this morning. Stubbed my toe on the end table, then stepped in dog poop, because the kids forgot to take the dog out again last night. Left the clothes in the washer, so I had to use the sniff test to find the least offensive pair of underwear. Head outside, and the radiator blew in the old Chevy, making me more than an hour late for work. Of course, the boss was waiting for me as I tried to sneak in. Just one of those days. Like every pigeon on the planet is circling above, waiting to take a dump on me. The boss breathin' down my neck. It's gonna cost more than eight hundred to get that piece of crap car back on the road, and I don't know how in hell I'm gonna pay for that. So, I stumble in the door, ready to explode, when I hear you scream; "You're home!" Then you run up and knock me back against the wall with kisses. Throw your arms around me, giggling like a little kid, and rubbing all over me like we ain't been married these last twelve years. Then, just as fast, you turn away, with that wonderfully wicked smile of yours, sayin' "Enough of that. Dinner's ready." And you leave me standin' there by the front door, wonderin' what did I ever do to deserve someone like you? And how lucky I was to have you there to make everything all right again… Of course, dinner was awful, 'cause you can't cook worth a damn. But I still feel pretty lucky...
All in all, turned out to be a pretty good day.

249.

Listen to me. This stops now. All of it. I don't know
what your brother did, or what's going on with you two,
but there's no way you are gonna ruin another holiday.
Last year was bad enough, with all that screaming and
swearing, and the mashed potato food fight that sent
Grandma Gertie to the hospital with gravy-induced
glaucoma. Now you two are gonna get along, or I swear
to crackers, I will duct-tape your hands and feet to those
kitchen chairs and force-feed you stuffing until Uncle
Tony passes out again. Now the turkey is defrosting in
the sink, your mom has taken her Xanax and bourbon,
and Cousin Bobby has gotten a one-day release from
Juvie just so we can all have this nice quiet family dinner.
You will not – I repeat, you will NOT make my ulcer
flare up this Thanksgiving. Or I swear to crackers,
neither of you will see Christmas again. You hear me?

250.

Hell's bells, aren't you the cute one? I was just sitting
there, drinking my beer and all…when suddenly, you
walked in and the whole room lit up. Like every head
turned to see what just happened. And there you were,
with that shy little smile of yours, not realizing your walk
about knocked me out of my chair. I said to myself,
there's someone who vibrates on a whole new frequency.
Someone who could make me rethink my life from the
socks up. So whatta you say? Can I buy you a drink?

251.

Did you hear about Jerry? Man, that was a shame. Came out of nowhere too. I guess you never know when your time is up. You're sitting there, wasting hours. Wasting years. Then BAM, you never see it coming. Suddenly, no years left to waste. Not even a few extra minutes to take back and do something meaningful with. Yeah. I wonder what Jerry was thinking at the end.
I'm bettin' he wished he never even took up drunk skydiving.

252.

No no no no no! Don't you dare do that! I'm serious! That is over the line. Way over the line! Crap on crackers, have you no heart? Have you no sympathy at all? You know I am on day nine-and-a-half of a raw root kale juice and cabbage vinegar fiber cleanse. Nine-and-a-half days! My stomach sounds like a wounded hippo, and it's impossible for me to be more than fifteen feet from a bathroom. I'm not sure whether my colon or my taste buds hate me more. And after nine-and-a-half days of gut-wrenching, mouth-twisting, appetite abuse and tongue torture, even the smell of normal food makes me feel like passing out. And then you come over with a dozen fresh-baked Dunkin Donuts?! And sit there with frosting on your face, munching a double-glazed chocolate bear claw right in front of me! You don't know how close to death you are now. You really don't!

253.

Oh! I love this song! Don't you love this song? I hear it on the radio in my car, and have to crank it up so loud the windows rattle. I don't really sing. Well, in the shower I do. I may never make it on The Voice, but in my car, with the music blasting, I am a superstar! A driving diva. American idol in a Toyota. Every pop, country and rock and roll fantasy rolled into one. Beyoncé asks for my autograph. Kanye hands over his Grammy to me. I know I can't carry a tune. Cats and small animals run away when I try to hit anything above a B flat. But isn't that the beauty of music? For three minutes, I can move like Jagger. Fall in love. Break some hearts. Be tough and sexy and just about everything I'm really not.
Oooh. Oooh turn it up! I love this part!

254.

I like you. I know we just met, but there's a real love connection here. Maybe it's your eyes, or your smile. Or that strange little way you squint when I move closer, like this. See you did it again! Just then. It's endearing. There's something about it that fills me with confidence. And hope. Like we were meant to be together. That you were meant to save my life. That every day since I was born I've been waiting for just this moment, to meet you here. That's kinda creepy, isn't it? I'm not really a stalker. Really. Hey! Where are you going?

255.

You can stop interviewing right now, sir, because the person sitting in front of you, right at this second, is perfect for this job. I am a self-starting, self-motivated team player. I get along with everyone, but can work, day and night alone in my cubicle without talking to another soul. I'm smart and aggressive, but not too pushy or obnoxious. Leadership material, but willing to pay my dues and scrub floors, if necessary. And I guarantee you, they will be the cleanest floors you ever saw. So clean, you can eat off them. Not to imply that you are the kind of person that eats off floors. That would be disgusting. Although whatever you choose to eat off of is entirely your decision, and I'm fine with that, and I, uh, only meant disgusting in the most positive sense. And, again, I'm not saying that you are in any way, disgusting because you are clearly…well, not in any way, no matter what you…uh…I um, think I'm going to shut up now…

256.

What? How dare you! I can't believe you would accuse me of such a thing. I would never do anything like that. I don't know how that ring ended up in my pocket. I'm sure it was an accident. That has been in my family for years. My grandmother gave it to me and…well, she had a habit of leaving the price tag on everything. And honestly, I have no idea how all that jewelry ended up in my pants. Someone else must have put it there. You just can't trust people these days, y'know?

257.

Here we go! It's your birthday and we're gonna have the
greatest party ever! I'm talkin' sheer awesomeness! We'll
invite everyone you know, maybe even everyone you
ever met! That can't be more than what? Twenty or
thirty thousand people? Okay, maybe that's a bit much,
so at least eighty, or maybe three or four old friends
from school. You know the geeky-nerdy ones that don't
hate you, or think you're like a total loser? And we'll
have balloons, and clowns! Except clowns scare me, with
those white faces and painted grins? So, no clowns, but
serious food festivities. Maybe Munch Munch Burgers
'cause they have that dollar menu. And I can shove a
candle in a Hostess cupcake, and it will be like super-
celebratory, with your three geeky-nerdy friends singing
Happy Birthday, while crunching on cheap eats. Doesn't
that sound significantly awesome?!

258.

Feel that? The way my heart's beating all wild and crazy?
You do that to me. Just that little look in your eye and
that sweet, sexy smile makes me feel like I'm bungie
jumping into Jell-O. Like everything in my life has been
leading up to this single, spectacular moment. Look at
me. I'm trembling like a puppy in the rain, and you
haven't even touched me yet. You haven't even tried to
touch me. And I am so ready to be yours. All you have to
do is ask. In fact, don't ask at all. Just…you know…

259.

Time flies. I know that's a cliché, but it really does. It goes by so fast. One day you have a life, a family you adore, with more dreams piling up every day. Then before you know it, ten or twenty years slip away without a trace. All the things you thought you'd have so much time to do…well, they moved from your To Do List, to your even bigger Regret List for never getting done. That's life. It flies by, and you never see it happening. So I want you to go out there and grab every one of your dreams as tightly as you can, and never let go. Don't you dare end up like me. Waiting for somebody to tell you what to do. Go out and do it while you're young and time is on your side. But remember…no matter how many degrees and PhDs you get. You are still my sweet little pumpkin baby. Now tuck in that shirt, give us a kiss, lift up that chin, and go out there and take over the world! But don't drive too fast... And be home by six. I'm making your favorite tonight. Tuna noodle casserole!

260.

Is this for me? How thoughtful of you! Oh…it's um, perfect. How did you know? Really, I love it. This is exactly what I wanted…except perhaps in a size I could actually wear. And maybe a color that wouldn't make me look like a diseased pumpkin at some kind of last century, tie-dye festival. But it's perfect. You shouldn't have. No, I really mean that. You shouldn't have…

261.

Why do I look like this? I look like this because I almost died today! Really. I'm lucky I made it here at all.

Last night was my best friend's birthday, and she talked me into six too many tequilas, like she always does. Of course, I knew today was a work day, so partying like a horny frat boy in a Judd Apatow movie was kind of crazy dumb, but you know when Lindsey starts her hooting and giggle-gulping, it's hard not to get caught up in the fun. Fortunately, I wasn't totally mind-numbed and called it a night at three AM. But that's not when I almost died.

When my alarm went off at six, I almost wished I had died, the way my head was feeling. Worst hangover ever! Or at least the worst hangover since the last time Lindsey and me got together.

So I slowly crawled on my hands and knees into the shower. Made sure I didn't slip in the tub, so I didn't almost die there either.

The shower actually cleared my head a little. At least enough for me to crack open my eyelids halfway. And that's when my second alarm goes off. The one I set to let me know I've only got fifteen minutes to get my butt out the door, or I'm going to be late for work again.

So I leap out of the shower and start my last-minute, mad-dash mirror routine. Blow-drying with my left hand, brushing my teeth with my right, and wrapping a towel around my foot to wipe my other leg at the same time. I've got it down to a science, and on a good day, I can be bus ready in six-point-two minutes…

Only this time, my half-closed eyes overshot the toothpaste and it squirted out all over the floor. There I was…hopping on one leg with the towel wrapped around my right foot, when my left foot hit that glob of Ultra-Bright and I feel myself going over. I'm falling in slow motion, but my mind is thinking; "Uh oh. Serious pain to follow." So I reach for the shower curtain, which does nothing to break my fall. Instead, it rips open and wraps around me, knocking my toothbrush to the back of my throat, and sending me sprawling backwards. The blow dryer drops straight into the toilet, and you know what happens when electricity and water mix. My arm is the only thing not wrapped up in the torn shower curtain, so my funny bone slams KERPLOW into the toilet seat, which hurts like hell, but probably saved me from having my head split open, or being electrocuted in the toilet bowl, which looks like a Roman candle, sending up this huge shower of sparks.

Now I'm lying there on the cold bathroom floor: toothpaste on my foot, wet towel scrunched between my legs, funny bone screaming in pain, and the rest of me wrapped like a sobbing burrito in what's left of my plastic shower curtain. That's when I smell something burning, and realize the sparks from the short-circuiting blow-dryer in the toilet caught my hair on fire, before blowing out all the circuit breakers for a three-block area. So, go on… Ask me again why I look like this! I dare you…

262.

I grew up in the strangest, craziest, most bizarre family.
Like they were almost from another planet. That's what it
felt like. I'd see them all sittin' around that table, chokin'
down tons of the greasiest, most disgusting food you
could imagine. Eatin' ten times more than the average
human could eat without exploding. And all the time,
they're yellin' and complainin' and laughin' like there was
no tomorrow. I'd stare at them whoopin' and hollerin'
and chokin' down all that food, and think "I must have
been adopted. "But let me tell you something… Those
people knew how to love. They knew how to set me
right, if I was goin' down the wrong path. And I knew
they had my back if anyone messed with me. So yeah,
maybe I was adopted, or dropped right in the middle of
some intergalactic freak show. But they were good
people where it counts. In the heart. But that don't mean
they weren't batshit crazy…

263.

I want this. I want it all. All of it. Every challenge. Every
bit of glory I can grab. I want it so badly I can taste it. I
want to chomp down on it and swallow it whole and let
it leak out my pores like some awesome rock concert
laser light show, stunning everybody with my artistry and
sheer brilliance! That's how much I want it! Yeah! Well,
yeah. I have had a few cups of Starbucks this morning.
Why do you ask?

264.

It's funny. All my life I have been looking for someone like you. Who likes what I do. Has the same tastes and interests. Loves the same kinds of food and has that same quirky sense of humor we share. We are so alike, I can't remember ever arguing with you, or disagreeing about anything. You always know what I'm thinking, and say yes to whatever I want to do. And that's why I am so bored to death with this relationship! I thought I wanted someone who would be easy to get along with, but come on now! I need a partner, not a clone. It's worth an argument now and then, just to see what happens. So, fight with me once in a while. Express an original idea. Show me something new. Challenge my expectations. Expand my horizons! Just not too much. Okay?

265.

I tell you what. I don't care if they are Republicreeps or Demokooks…them fat-cat talk-doctors in Congress ain't worth one swallow's worth of spit. They only got two jobs – to let our boys scare the bejeezes outa any nutbuckets that threaten our country and pass some sort of common-sense budget afore this country goes down the drain in a gold-plated handbasket. It ain't rocket science. You take in this much, that's all you got to spend. You ain't got enough, you cut back or do without. That's what every straight-talkin' American's been doing since I don't know when. Like I said, them Congress folk ain't worth a swallow's worth of spit. No sireee.

266.

Mom, Dad, I've got something to tell you. You better sit
down because…well, I know how you both get.

You know how you always wanted me to be like
everyone else in the family? To go into the family
business like Freddy and Martha and Jack, then settle
down with someone you approve of, and crank out a ton
of grandchildren for you to spoil? I know that's your
dream, and that you only want the best for me. I know
you've been pushing me towards Wanda Jenkins ever
since elementary school. Telling me every day what a
good wife she'd make…

But…I'm sorry, but that's not me. That's not the life I
want. I tried, but I just don't fit into that lifestyle. The
truth is… I'm smart. Really smart. Like Harvard law
school smart. And I just don't see myself working in the
Quickie Suds for the rest of my life. I mean, coin-
operated laundry is fine for Freddy and Martha and Jack,
but it's not me. I want to be a Supreme Court Justice,
and maybe invent an app that uses complex algorithms
to apply Constitutional law principles to international
treaties and financial transactions. And Wanda Jenkins is
really sweet and all, but we all know she's as dumb as a
year-old potato. I mean, can you see her married to a
tech entrepreneur and Supreme Court Justice?

Mom, Dad, I know you're disappointed I got that full
scholarship to Harvard and then the internship at that
prestigious Wall Street firm. But I can't keep living a lie. I
can't deny who I am. Please don't cry. Please?

267.

O.M.G., it's you! You're you, aren't you? You were in that movie! The one with that guy, and all those other guys. You liked him, but he dumped you because you weren't half as good looking as the star. And then you were in that other movie, you know. The really crazy bad one with that big furry alligator, or alien rabbit monster, whatever it was. You know, the one that won the award for "Dumbest Movie of All Time?" And you got chewed up by the big furry alligator, or alien bunny before you could even say a line. That was so crazy! Hey, can you take a selfie with me, making that same silly face you made right before you were eaten? No, it was dopier than that. You had drool coming out of your mouth. Yeah, like that! I am such a big fan. What was your name again?

268.

Don't make a big deal of it. I'm sure you'd do the same for me if the situations were reversed. I know you would. To be perfectly honest…I need to do this for you. I need to do this for me, too. I need to prove to myself that I'm the kind of person who would put it all on the line for a friend. That despite all the crap I throw around, maybe I'm really not that two-faced and cold-hearted after all. That I'm a better person than everybody says I am. That I might even be a better person than maybe I think I am. Anyway, it's no big thing.
That's why we have two kidneys, anyway

269.

It's not what you're thinking. Really. I don't want you to jump to conclusions and have your usual panic attacks, where your imagination outruns reality. Like when you think you know everything I'm going to say, even before I get the first three words out of my mouth.

Please, just let me say my piece, and try to listen for once. That's all I ask. Just listen to what I have to say...

The bottom line is...I'm done here. I can't do this anymore. I look at you, and all I can think about is all those wasted years. The missed opportunities. All the smiles that will never be thrown my way, while day after day, I'm forced to look at your sorry face.

I'm sorry. I know that was harsh. But it's not what you think. There isn't anybody else. I'm not running into the arms of someone better. I'm just running away from you. Let's face it... You and I are relationship roadkill, and there are only so many times I can have my wants and desires splattered all over the freeway like some grotesque piece of modern art.

But you really shouldn't blame yourself for this disaster of a relationship. It's not you. It's me.

Maybe I'm not built for a real relationship. Maybe I'm not strong, or smart, or mature enough to make it work. And...What?

Oh...so that *is* what you were thinking?

270.

I will do well in History this year. I will do well in History this year. I will not care that the teacher is as exciting as a cadaver from the Civil War era. Or that the Ancient Greeks were perverts who walked around in togas that looked like bedsheets, and this one guy named Alex called himself 'The Great,' because he stabbed more people with spears than stabbed him back. Okay, so maybe they invented democracy and the Olympics and all that, but they also believed in these real cranky gods that would create bizarre things, like minotaurs and cyclopses. So how smart could they really be, huh? And don't get me started about the Romans! They didn't dress much better, and had their own set of crazy things like gladiators and stuff. But I will do well in History. Because the very last thing I want to do is have to take it again next year! Because there'll be even more History by then!

271.

Why, hello! Thank you so much for coming over! You look wonderful, you really do. I don't believe anybody would ever know that you... I'm so sorry... I always say the wrong thing. It's just that I was so worried about you. We all were. And to see you suddenly show up at my door after all this time. And especially after all that happened... Well, it means so much to me. But look at me. I have forgotten my manners. Please come in. Dry off, have a seat and let's catch up on everything.
So tell me... How was prison?

272.

Dear Lord, it sure has been a long time since you last heard from me. You know I'm not much good at prayin'. Guess I don't practice half as much as I should. And I ain't got no doubt there are a whole lot of better people you'd rather spend your time talkin' to. Like that Pope guy, or some of those fancy-haired TV preachers with the booming voices and expensive suits.

But if you don't mind sparin' a few extra minutes, I'd like to toss a few words your way.

Now, you're probably thinking I'm gonna start beggin' for something like most folks I know. But I'm not. I don't need to hit the lottery or nothin' like that. And, yeah, I'd kinda like to be a decade or two younger, and lose this beer belly, but we both know that ain't never gonna happen. You and me both know I earned every inch of gut flab I'm carryin' these days.

So, all in all, I'm good. But if you're still up there listenin', I'd just like to thank you for takin' time away from all that creatin', and blessin' me with that crazy lady of mine, who for some strange reason, is still crazy about me. We both know I don't deserve her, but thank God, the woman hasn't realized that yet.

So until she does, I'm here to say I will cherish every single second you give me with that lady. Good times or bad. Whatever you see fit to throw at us.

Guess that's 'bout all I got to say. Except great job on kittens…bourbon…Aruba…and the universe.

Keep up the good work. Amen.

273.

Here are some things you should know about me... I like hot, steamy showers and stealing an extra hour of sleep in the morning, even if I have a jillion things on my To Do List. My guilty pleasures are casual flirting, macaroni and cheese, stupid comedies and laughing for no reason at all. I enjoy stretching like a cat, big fuzzy sweaters fresh out of the dryer, soft red sunsets by the beach, and catching someone staring at me out of the corner of my eye. I adore giggling children, stealing fries, and smiling at strangers, just to confuse them. I like dance crazy, act silly, adore deep philosophical discussions and spontaneous displays of affection. I never settle, never share my food, and never lose an argument. If you can handle all that, I just might let you fall in love with me.

274.

So, when the spaceship landed...yeah, the spaceship. A real, outside-this-galaxy circular thing, with this brain melting sound and strange glowing lights and this fog pouring out of it like you see in the movies kind of thing. Know what I'm saying? I'm right there and this thing from another planet hovers over my head for maybe four seconds, then plops right down in my driveway right next to where I'm standing. Only I wasn't really standing at that point, I was more sort of face first in the mud, because I'd had a few at the tailgate party and... but that had absolutely nothing to do with it! I know what I saw, and I can't wait to tell those TV people all about it!

275.

Listen, you know how I like to gamble. Lots of people
do. Just about everybody I know. I mean, what's wrong
with a little card game now and then? Even the
government has lotteries. The government! So how bad
could it be?

I can hold my own in a card game. But what kills me are
the slots. They're all shiny and colorful and loud, and
sometimes they call out to you, like those "Wheel of
Fortune' machines you can hear all over the casino.
"Wheel – Of – Fortune!" Anyway, it's fun. And I only
bring as much money as I can afford to lose. So, what's
wrong with that?

The trouble is now they let you use your debit cards right
in the casino. And then credit cards, once you run out of
money in your bank account, y'know what I'm saying?
So, the other week, I was down at the Golden Jackpot,
and I had this major hot streak going. You should have
been there. I'm hitting everything. Cherries, bars, lucky
sevens, and even the Wheel of Fortune extra spins. I was
on the roll of a lifetime! And everybody knows, when
you have a roll, you gotta play it out, am I right?

Well, wouldn't you know, the machine goes cold, and I'm
down a bit. Then a bit more. And before I knew it, both
my debit and credit cards are maxed out.

So that's why I can't pay my rent this month. But don't
you worry. I'll get it to you next week. I'm going back to
the casino and I know my luck's gonna change real soon.
I can feel it.

276.

You're walking down the street, when one day it hits you. More than half the people passing by are younger than you. You look around and realize most of the planet is younger than you too. When did that happen? Late at night, you stare into the mirror, and there's your father's face staring back at you. Worry lines, hairline creeping to the top of your head, dull eyes shocked by time. Stores and restaurants start calling you 'sir,' with the same condescending respect you used to use on clueless old-timers. You work for bosses ten or twenty years younger than you, and they know you aren't the hotshot anymore. The one with the ideas. You're the deadwood, marking time until retirement. They're at the beginnings of their careers, while you're sliding towards the finale. The wrap up. They have a life left to squander, while you tie up loose ends as best you can, on that long, downward spiral to corporate obsolescence... Yeah, I just got the notice about my next high school reunion. How did you know?

277.

You have no right to think like that. No right at all. I didn't start this. You pursued me. You used all your charm, and that gorgeous smile of yours. And you kept coming, no matter how hard I tried not to fall in love with you. So, it's your fault. I'm here with you now, and this is where I'm gonna stay. You better get used to it.

278.

What's that, officer? No, I don't know why you pulled
me over. I stopped at the red light…or would have, if I
hadn't been going so fast. You know how hard it is to
stop when you're going eighty… Uh, I mean thirty. I
think my speedometer is busted. I guess your radar must
be broken too, because there was absolutely *no way* I was
going over fifty. I mean, thirty-five. It's just that the
streets around here are so narrow, and all those people
were standing right in the middle of the road… What do
you mean, I was the driving on the sidewalk? Are you
sure? Well, what's the speed limit for the sidewalk? 'Cuz I
know I wasn't going over sixty… I mean, twenty-five….

279.

Christmas was lame this year. I remember when it used
to be so much fun, all those presents and everything.
Tearing wrapping paper and making a mess, opening up
all those toys and cool things. It was even worth
pretending I still believed in Santa Claus, which to tell the
truth, I still kinda do. But now, Christmas is no fun at all.
It's like two toys, lots of clothes and a few gift cards from
aunts and uncles I haven't seen for years. Even Mom and
Dad give me gift cards now, like it's too much trouble to
shop for me anymore. You know how long it takes to
unwrap a gift card? Two seconds. And then you have to
act surprised, like I have absolutely no idea what this flat
little rectangular package could possibly be. Adults…they
sure take all the fun out of Christmas, you know?

280.

First dates are so uncomfortable, don't you agree? Both people trying desperately to show themselves in the best light, and truth is the only casualty. Like peacocks strutting around with someone else's feathers. It's only after you are together for a while you realize how exaggerated those first date conversations really were. So, I suggest we tell all our lies up front and get them out of the way, okay?

Great. Then I'll start...

I'm an amateur nuclear physicist and sole heir to the throne of Sweden. I'm four inches taller than I look, a decade younger than I appear, and far wiser than I ever imagined I'd be. I'm listed in the Guinness Book of World Records for stationary bungee jumping, and was awarded an Oscar last year for Best Nostrils in a Dramatic Feature. I play miniature golf every Saturday with Hillary Clinton, Justin Bieber, and the Pope, who has sometimes been known to cheat on his score card. I purchased a small Latin American country, but only get to visit it occasionally. Many of my body parts are patent pending. I'm working on the Great American Novel, but it's not finished yet, because I'm writing it in five different languages at once, and those Chinese picture-letters can be a real bitch. In my free time, I darn socks, design US currency, and knit my own trash bags.

I believe that about covers it...

Now you lie to me.

.

281.

Man, I shoulda decked him! Right then and there, I shoulda hauled back and tossed a serious right cross straight into that ugly, condescending pie hole of' his! I coulda done it to! I coulda laid him out flat, and I'm betting half the people in that office would have stood up and slapped me on the back, like I was king of the world. That's how much they hate that guy. And how much I hate that guy. So what if he's younger and has biceps and pecs the size of a credenza? I'm betting the years since he was a champion caged fighter have caught up with him. And since Newton defines force as mass times acceleration, all I have to do is set this beer belly in motion and he's toast. Serious toast.

282.

What the hell is wrong with you, huh? Look at you... You're smart, funny, and so good-looking it's unfair. You dance, give massages, and get along with all my friends. Even the ones I don't like. You cook Italian and Chinese, and your soft, sexy kisses make my eyes roll back in my head. So how are you still single? What are you? Some kind of fascist kleptomaniac, booger-eating conspiracy nut, with a mommy complex? That's it, isn't it? You're a fascist kleptomaniac, booger-eating conspiracy nut, with a mommy complex! Because if you *aren't* any of those things, I am sooo moving in with you next week. And I will expect Chicken Marsala, Swedish massages and long passionate kisses from now on. You okay with that?

283.

So I stumble out of bed, trying to rub the sleep from my eyes, squeezing as much comfort as I can out of my morning coffee, when suddenly the dog runs up to me and says "Hey, you forgot to put water in my dish!" With absolutely no consideration for how foggy headed I am this early in the morning. So I...

What? Yeah, that's what my dog said.

Well, he didn't actually *say* that, but I knew that's what he was thinking. I guess I have this ability to connect with dogs. All pets really. Know what they're thinking, with all those barks and chirps and roars and things.

It's true. Mostly dogs think about food, squirrels, or when and where to poop. Cats...? They're a lot harder to read, because they usually don't have that much to say. Always think they're so far above you, there's no reason to share with you anyway. But as I was saying, he scampers in and says...

No, I'm serious. I really talk to dogs. It's people I have trouble communicating with. Like the fact that you keep interrupting me when I'm trying to tell you about my morning.

So why don't you SIT and STAY like a GOOD BOY...
...and just let me finish my story?

Now where was I...?

Oh, yeah. My dog says to me...

284.

Look, I know you feel bad. Life has let you down and there's nobody you can turn to. And maybe it feels like it isn't even worth getting out of bed in the morning, 'cause it's just gonna be one disappointment after another. Whoever said life was gonna be easy? Life is pain. It's heartache and despair and watching one dream after another crumble in the dust for no rhyme or reason. It's people breaking promises, and never being around when you really need 'em. It's having your heart ripped out of your chest, because the love of your life doesn't even know you exist, or if she does, she thinks she can do a hellova lot better than you, and has no problem telling you so. It's jobs you hate, bills you can't pay, and random idiots crushing all the hope out of you. All you can do is brush your teeth and hope to hell nothing kills you while you sleep. So, put your toys away and man up, kid. You're six years old now. It only gets worse from here.

285.

So, when I touch my nose like this, the coast is clear. When I scratch my chin, it means they're watching us. When I crack my knuckles, it means the price is too low. If I choke on my own spit, the price is too high. If I run my fingers through my hair with my left hand, it means get ready. If I do the same with my right, the deal is off, and we better get out of there. And if I sneeze three times, it means I need a tissue... My allergies are real bad this time of year. Got all that? Okay, then, let's do this...

286.

Touch me. All I want is for you to touch me. Soft and gentle, like you mean it. Don't paw at me like some awkward grizzly taking massage lessons. Just take your fingertips and slowly slide them down my cheek. Tender as a kiss. Just like that. Now feel the warmth of my lips. Notice how your teasing touch starts to make my breath rise and fall. Memorize each curve of my face, my chin and my neck with your soft, caressing fingers. It's all there. Everything you need to know. Everything you want to draw out of me. It's all there in that one sweet, sensuous touch. That's it. That's the way. That's…ohhh!

287.

See this? This is my ticket outta this dump. The Jackpot's up to $123 million and I already know how I'm gonna spend it. First off, I'm gonna walk right into the boss's office and quit my job. No, better still, I'm gonna buy the company, and fire his sorry butt! That'll teach him to complain about me taking too many sick days. Then I'm gonna pay off some debts. Buy a Lamborghini or two. Get me a house in Italy and maybe even a private island. Guess I'll haveta give my ex a grand just to shut her up, and then a few hundred to all my relatives who never liked me much anyway. Then a trip around the world with Hollywood starlets. Record my own music video. Be the next big thing. Yup, these Powerball numbers are my ticket outta here. I can't wait 'til the drawing tonight!

288.

You know what you need in your life? A big healthy dose
of ME! Feeling down? I'll be there to cheer you up.
Anxious and upset? Count on me to soothe you with
tender touches and loving smiles. And when you're all
pumped up because that last big deal went through, and
all these giddy groupies pop out of nowhere… gushing
that you're the new king of the world…well, then you'll
need me to knock some perspective back into your head.
Let you know that you're appreciated, not for what you
do, but for who you are. Because when the parasites and
paparazzi drift away in search of the next big thing – and
they will – I'll still be your biggest fan. I know I may not
look like much. But I am the only one who knows you,
loves you, and who is willing to stand beside you, whatever happens. I may not be as flashy, or young, or as
exciting as all the others…but I am all you need. And it's
about time you open those beautiful eyes and realized it.

289.

Can someone please tell me why women prefer to go to
the bathroom in a group? There's nothing about standing
in front of a porcelain receptacle that makes me wish I
had a crowd around to share the experience. And how do
they do that anyway? Do they synchronize their bladders
or something? "Okay, we'll hit the rest room at precisely
10:22. Drink a large glass of water… *now!*"
Maybe men were never meant to understand women. But
maybe that's what makes them so damn interesting…

290.

Mom. Dad... I need to tell you something. Something important. I think you better sit down. This has been weighing on me for a long time, so please don't interrupt, okay? First off... I love you, and nothing is ever going to change that. I know you've always had this vision of how my life should go. College. A respectable career as a doctor that you could brag to your friends about. You expected me to settle down and get married, giving you lots of giggly grandchildren. Maybe buy a house down the street, with the stereotypical white picket fence. And I did try... I tried hard to be the person you wanted me to be. But that's not who I am. That's not the kind of life that would make me happy. That's not who I have to be. Whew...this is harder than I thought. So, I'm just going to come right out and say it... Mom. Dad. I'm going to be an actor. I'm going to follow this dream wherever it leads me. However long it takes. Why are you smiling? What did you think I was going to tell you?

291.

In Neverland news today, Peter Pan files for divorce, terminating his twelve-year marriage to famed starlet Tinkerbell. It seems Pan was enraged at Miss Bell's posing nude for the centerfold of Playbug Magazine. When approached for comment, Tinkerbell replied; "Peter? He'll never grow up."

292.

Now before you go and start tearin' up on me, let me clue you in on something. There's one thing I can't stand…one thing I don't tolerate, and that's weakness. Any kind of weakness. Don't like the thought of it. Don't like the smell of it. I don't like the way it insults my presence with all those quivering little insecurities. I don't allow even the slightest hint of weakness in myself, and I sure as hell don't put up with it in others. It sets me off big time. That timid look in the corner of their eyes, as if they're terrified I'm gonna bark at them or somethin'… I see that look, and it makes me want to grab a rock and just go to town on their skull and… Well, like I said…it sets me off. So, you think about that before you start whining or complaining. Think about it real good.
But we're getting off track here. This is your appointment, not mine. And we've already eaten up the first ten minutes of your therapy session. So, lie down on the couch and tell me... What brings you in today?

293.

Dear friends, we are gathered here to say a final farewell to Milton Spelk. Many remember Milt as an average guy, occasional worker, loveless husband and weekend father. Yet, Milt always believed we should never regret mistakes we make in life. If he was alive today, he would tell us not to mourn him. We shouldn't cry over life's passing troubles. So, I say to you now, in words that may seem strangely familiar... Don't cry over Milt Spelk.

294.

Eeew... What is it with these like, skuzzy old men trying to hit on high school girls? My best friend's dad tries to act all slick and smiley whenever I go over to her house. It's like most of the time he shlumps around, like a Baggie filled with water. But as soon as he sees me, he like, grows a spine and amps up the like he's 'O.D.'ing on some super energy six pack. His eyes get all big and happy, and he leans in close and asks me about school, and who I'm dating and even the music I like, as if he had a clue. Like he's never even heard of Mange Party or the Desiccated Earlobes! He's that ancient! I'm talking Civil War-type fossildom. I mean, he's like at least thirty! Seriously. It just creeps me out.

295.

Tragedy struck in Fairyland as an initially peaceful demonstration resulted in the death of a student. Demonstrators gathered to protest the bussing of puppets and marionettes to Fairyland High School. As the puppets filed off the bus, they were harassed by the angry mob, who chanted, "No dummies at Fairyland High!" Protestors surrounded one student named Pinocchio, and in an act of indescribable brutality, picked up the wooden puppet and shoved him into a pencil sharpener. Papa Geppetto, the puppet's creator, arrived on the scene only to find a pile of shavings and a pointy stub. Geppetto avoided reporters, and Pinocchio himself was unavailable for comment.

296.

Lullaby and good-night La la la la la la la...

I wish there was a way I could burn this image into my brain. Make a permanent mental record of this face...this feeling...this moment...

You look up at me with those big dark eyes, and I have absolutely no idea what you're thinking. I don't even know if you can think at only three weeks old. But here you are, in my arms. My girl. My baby girl.

You made me love you I didn't want to do it Didn't want to do it...

I have a confession to make. I never thought I could love anything so completely. But when you came into my life, everything changed. You were so tiny, so helpless, so totally mine.

It was easy when it was just me and your Mommy. I didn't have to worry so much about screwing up, because Mommy is really smart, and I knew we would always be able to bounce back, no matter what I did.

But with you here, things are different. Now I have to face a lifetime of worries, that I will do the right things, say the right words that help you grow up happy and healthy and trauma-free. Words that will keep you loving me as much as I love you at this very moment.

Is this the little girl I carried? Is this the little boy at play? I don't remember growing older, when did they?

You may not believe this, but some day, you're going to grow up and leave me. You're going to find someone else to love, and leave your old Daddy far behind...

I'll probably be old and gray by then, and I'll cry as I walk you down the aisle. I promise you, I will be the happiest man on Earth when you get married. And the saddest...

It's funny, I've only had you for three weeks, and suddenly, I can't imagine life without you.

Seedlings turn overnight to sunflower blossoming even as they grow...

Hey! That was a smile, wasn't it?! Did you just smile for Daddy? You did, didn't you?!

Oh, Lord, please let me burn this image into my brain, so for the rest of my life I can remember what it's like to hold this little, precious thing in my arms.

Oh, big old yawn. I'm boring you, aren't I? That's okay. You'll get used to it.

For now, you just close those big, beautiful eyes and go to sleep.

Everything will be all right. Daddy's here.

Daddy's here...

Lullaby and good-night La la la la la la la...

297.

There is nothing sexier than a super nerdy techno geek with the ultra-latest iPhone talking edged-out apps code. I go to the Apple store almost every week, so I can digitally sigh over all that maxed out hardware and flying graphics. I mean, a girl's gotta have her phone, and those brain-enhanced blue shirts at the genius bar really bring it. But whenever my Mom tags along, she is so last century clunky, saying "Why do I need that?" and not even knowing the diff between apps and programs. The poor thing thinks texting is like soooo current calendar, I'm almost embarrassed for her. It's hard to believe she popped me out all those years ago!

298.

Do you believe in fate? Like this moment was meant to be? Like in some great cosmic plan, I was meant to be sitting right here, in this very seat, when you walked by and sat in that very seat there, and then looked up from your book and noticed me?

Okay, so maybe I had to clear my throat a few times to get your attention. And when that didn't work, I had to tap my pen on the table a couple of dozen times or more. And when your nose was still buried in that book, maybe I had to accidentally spill half my cup of mocha latte on you, so that you'd look up as you were wiping the hot coffee of your lap. But maybe that's how it was meant to be. It's our destiny to meet like this. Isn't fate funny?

299.

Aaaaaargggh! Is it encoded somewhere in their DNA for men to be completely oblivious to everything?! Do they have an 'inability to put a toilet seat down' gene? Is there a 'burp and scratch' chromosome scientists haven't discovered yet? Some kind of evolutionary defect that makes them totally unable to understand that sometimes a woman needs to talk about something OTHER than how bad the Red Sox are pitching this year, or who rushed for how many yards against who knows what team? Honestly, if they didn't look so damn cute and clueless, I'd say do away with the whole gender and the world would be a better place! But maybe science will find a cure for male patterned madness before I bury my husband in the backyard. At least we can hope.

300.

Before we take this any further, let me give you the basics and ground rules...

One: Don't expect anything from me. I'm not a giver and I'm not into compassion or compatibility. My relationships go one way.

Two: I am shallow, egotistical and narcissistic. I want non-stop flattery, and I expect you to mean it. Tell me every day how impressive I am. How smart and how talented.

Three: Make me the center of your world, and we'll get along just fine.

So, what do you say? Am I seriously cute, or what?

About The Author

Vin Morreale, Jr. is an award-winning screenwriter, acting teacher, casting director and internationally produced playwright.

Vin was a founding member of the San Francisco Playwrights Center and the Senseless Bickering Comedy Theatre. He has directed hundreds of works for stage, screen and radio across the country.

As president of *Vin Morreale Casting,* along with his nationally known *Burning Up The Stage* acting workshops, he has helped nearly 30,000 actors find work in movies, TV, stage and video.

Vin was awarded the prestigious *Al Smith Writing Fellowship*, and his scripts, stage plays, documentaries, museum exhibits and radio comedy have received hundreds of productions around the world, as well as being translated into Chinese, Italian, Russian and Spanish.

Vin has sold material to network and cable television networks, had feature screenplays optioned and produced, and his work has been seen in more than 15 countries. He was named a top screenwriter by both The International Screenwriters Association and The Blacklist.org.

You can find more of his books at *academyartspress.com.*

And be sure to check out the exciting opportunities at *300monologues.com.*

CPSIA information can be obtained
at www.ICGtesting.com
Printed in the USA
FSHW021533261018

9 780999 147337